HAND ME DOWNS

Just Because They Gave Them

To You Doesn't Mean You

Have To Wear Them

What to do with

Generational Iniquity

Rob Thorpe

First published by All In Ministries, Inc. October 15, 2024

Printed in the United States of America

For more information, contact All In Ministries, Inc. at
marriagesthatmatter@gmail.com

Cover design by Chris Paxton at Paxton Creative Resources

DEDICATION

To my amazing, God-fearing, patient, loving, supportive wife of nearly fifty years! God handcrafted you and deliberately brought us together to share this amazing journey, and I can't think of anyone I would have rather experienced it with. It has always been you!

And to our wonderful, encouraging friends Hal and Barbara Hillman and our entire small group - Jerry and Sherri Byrum, Merlin and Rita Hagan, Ken and Amber Singleton, and Tim and Tammy Fielder. You guys have prayed, cried, and laughed with us for years and we couldn't have enjoyed (or needed) it more.

To my amazing mother, who tirelessly and sacrificially raised my brother and me. She always put our needs before hers, encouraged and prayed for us, and was God's primary instrument to bring us to a relationship with Him. Our family would not be who we are or where we are without your prayers and your example of a godly Christian life.

TABLE OF CONTENTS

Introduction 7

Chapter 1 - Like Father, Like Son................................9

Chapter 2 - Not Necessarily 15

Chapter 3 - Nothing But The Blood 21

Chapter 4 - The Main Thing 29

Chapter 5 - Sound Familiar?......................................39

Chapter 6 - Discovery 53

Chapter 7 - Confess, Repent, Renounce 61

Chapter 8 - Forgiveness - Family 67

Chapter 9 - Forgiveness - Others 77

Chapter 10 - Forgiveness - Me 83

Chapter 11 - Suit Up 95

Chapter 12 - A Wartime Mentality...........................109

Chapter 13 - With Your Boots On 121

Conclusion 129

Appendix A 131

Appendix B.. 136

INTRODUCTION

For over 30 years, (1976-2009), legendary broadcaster and radio personality Paul Harvey's ultra-popular radio program, The Rest of the Story, arrested listeners' attention. Mr. Harvey would tell a short story regarding little-known facts about a person, place, company, or time in history, but held back a key piece of the story (similar to a punchline of a joke), until the very end of the broadcast. It was only then that he would reveal the fascinating, missing piece and announce his famous tagline in closing - "and now you know, the REST of the story".

The reasoning behind writing what is essentially a sequel to my first book on spiritual warfare, "**Victorious**", is two-fold:

1. Spiritual warfare is fought on multiple fronts and only one of those was discussed in Victorious. We are exhorted to put on armor, take up weapons, and engage in "hand-to-hand combat" (wrestle) with our mortal enemy. All of these speak of an in-your-face, frontal assault battlefield. Victorious was intended to shed light on who this enemy really is, what his "schemes"/tactics are, and how to recognize and overcome them. There is much more to the story than could be included in that single volume.

2. Believers need to know - The Rest of the Story! There is a second theater of battle that hides in the shadows. Unlike the American Civil War where opposing armies simply lined up on opposite ends of a battlefield, in broad daylight, and marched

toward each other firing their weapons - this type of spiritual combat more resembles the Vietnam War, where opponents fought in thick jungles filled with snipers, booby-traps and hidden soldiers. By the time you recognize their presence, you have most likely already been wounded.

No matter what your religious belief, or whether you have a belief at all - your physical, emotional, and spiritual lives are deeply impacted by the lives and choices of the relatives who came before you.

Understanding this reality can provide us with significant insight into our inclinations toward certain sinful tendencies and behavior patterns. Once we recognize them for what they are, we can take steps to get rid of those hand-me-downs once and for all.

So if the Son sets you free, you will be free indeed.
John 8:36

CHAPTER 1

LIKE FATHER, LIKE SON

Our families have the greatest influence on our development, including the development of our patterns of sin.

Jonathan Edwards was a Puritan Preacher in the 1700s. He was one of the most respected preachers of his day. He attended Yale at the age of thirteen and later went on to become the president of Princeton College. He married his wife Sara in 1727 and they were blessed with eleven children. Every night when Mr. Edwards was home, he would spend an hour conversing with his family and then praying a blessing over each child. Jonathan and his wife Sarah passed on a great, godly legacy to their eleven children.

An American educator, A.E. Winship decided to trace the descendants of Jonathan Edwards almost 150 years after his death. His findings are remarkable, especially when compared to another man from the same period known as Max Jukes.

Jonathan Edwards' legacy includes: 1 U.S. Vice-President, 1 Dean of a law school, 1 dean of a medical school, 3 U.S. Senators, 3 governors, 3 mayors, 13 college presidents, 30 judges, 60 doctors, 65 professors, 75 Military officers, 80 public office holders, 100 lawyers, 100 clergymen, and 285 college graduates.

Can this be explained as simply good luck or coincidence?

Edwards was a godly man, but he was also hard-working, intelligent, and moral. Furthermore, Winship states, "Much of the capacity and talent, intensity and character of the more than 1,400 of Edwards' family is due to Mrs. Edwards."

Max Jukes' legacy came to people's attention when the family trees of 42 different men in the New York prison system were traced back to him. He lived in New York at about the same period as Edwards. Jukes' descendants included: 7 murderers, 60 thieves, 190 prostitutes, 150 other convicts, 310 paupers, and 440 who were physically wrecked by addiction to alcohol. Of the 1,200 descendants that were studied, 300 died prematurely.

These contrasting legacies provide an example of what sociologists call the five-generation rule. "How a parent raises their child — the love they give, the values they teach, the emotional environment they offer, the education they provide — influences not only their children but the four generations to follow, either for good or evil."

There are multiple examples of this truth in the Bible.

The most familiar, and most devastating, is the fall of Adam and Eve (the ancestors of us all) in the Garden of Eden. Because of their disobedience to God's one and only commandment, (**Genesis 2:16-**

17), every human being ever born has been born under (inherited) the curse of sin.

"Therefore, just as through one man sin entered into the world, and death through sin, and so death (separation from God) spread to all men because all sinned". **Romans 5:12**

Another, less devastating to all mankind story, is the story of how Abram (Abraham) and his son, Isaac, both used deception and lies to save themselves at the risk of their wives.

Twice in Scripture, Abram said that his wife Sarai was his sister. And later, his son, Isaac, did the same with his own wife. The first time this happened (**Genesis 12**) was after Abram left Haran at 75 years old. While Abram, Sarai, and their tribe traveled around Canaan, he received a promise from God that He would give this land to Abram's descendants. Soon after, a famine struck the land. So Abram went down to Egypt to sojourn there, for the famine was severe in the land.

As they approached the powerful empire of Egypt, Abram made an unusual request of his wife: He said to Sarai, "I know that you are a beautiful woman, and when the Egyptians see you, they will say, 'This beautiful woman is his wife.' Then they will kill me, but let you live. But, if you say you are my sister, then it may go well with me because of you, and my life may be spared for your sake".

Motivated by selfish fear, Abram asked her to say that she was his sister, rather than his wife. What he feared came to pass - When Abram entered Egypt, the Egyptians saw that Sarai was indeed very beautiful, and when the princes of Pharaoh saw her, they praised her to Pharaoh, and she was taken into Pharaoh's house.

Abram was treated very well because of this and was given gifts of sheep, donkeys, camels, and servants. But, all was not right in Egypt: Sarai was Abram's wife, and God was not pleased. So the Lord afflicted Pharaoh and his house with great plagues because of what they did, and Pharaoh figured out something was amiss.

So Pharaoh called Abram and said, "What is this you have done to me? Why did you not tell me that she was your wife? Why did you say, 'She is my sister,' so that I took her for my wife? Now then, take your wife and go." Pharaoh ordered his men to send Abram, Sarai, and all his tribe out of Egypt".

Years passed, and Abram's name was changed by God from Abram to Abraham, meaning "father of many" to remind him of the promise that God had made to him, saying, "You shall be the father of a multitude of nations." (Genesis 17) And, God reiterated His promise to make a nation from Sarai, and changed her name to Sarah.

Despite God's continued protection and provision for Abraham, he repeated the same, wife-sister deception as before. This time, it took place after he witnessed the destruction of Sodom and Gomorrah and decided to move further away. So he travels down to the Philistine city of Gerar. Motivated by the same fear and selfish desire for self-preservation, he once again said of Sarah - "She is my sister", so as you would expect, Abimelech king of Gerar sent and took Sarah.

Thankfully, God intervened - again.

God warned Abimelech in a dream and said to him, "Behold, you are a dead man because of the woman whom you have taken, for she is a man's wife." Now Abimelech had not approached her, so he said, "Lord, will you kill an innocent people? Did he not himself say to me, 'She is my sister'? And she herself said, 'He is my brother.' In the integrity of my heart and the innocence of my hands, I have done this."

King Abimelech rose early the next morning and took swift action. Abimelech called Abraham and said to him, "What have you done to us? And how have I sinned against you, that you have brought on me and my kingdom a great sin? You have done to me things that ought not to be done." Abraham said, "I did it because I thought, 'There is no fear of God at all in this place, and they will kill me because of my wife.' Besides, she is indeed my sister, the daughter of my father though not the daughter of my mother, and she became my wife." While Abraham offered the pensive explanation that Sarah was, at least partially, his sister, his words did not erase the fact that he had deceived the king into believing Sarah was not his wife.

Fast forward to Genesis 26 and the story of Abraham's son, Isaac, who, as a result of another famine, traveled with his wife, Rebekah, to the same Gerar. Ironically, the king was none other than Abimelech, but most scholars believe Abimelech, II (son of Abraham's Abimelech).

Driven by the same lack of faith and abundance of self-preserving fear, Isaac uses deception/lying to cover his backside.

Isaac settled in Gerar, but when the men of the place asked him about his wife, he said, "She is my sister," for he feared to say, "My wife," thinking, "lest the men of the place should kill me because of Rebekah," because she was very attractive.

And when Abimelech, the king of the Philistines, looked out a window and saw Isaac and Rebekah laughing together, he called for Isaac and said, "Behold, she is your wife. How then could you say, 'She is my sister'?" Isaac said to him, "Because I thought, 'Lest I die because of her.'" Abimelech said, "What is this you have done to us? One of the people might easily have lain with your wife, and you would have brought guilt upon us." So Abimelech warned all the people, saying, "Whoever touches this man or his wife shall surely be put to death."

Isaac had not learned from the errors of his father even though God had intervened both times. Without God's intervention, both Abraham and Isaac could have lost their beautiful wives, along with God's promise that He would give this land to Abraham's descendants.

Abraham was a good man who, in many respects is worthy of emulation. Yet, even the Father of the Faith committed sins that were "visited upon" his son. Like all children, Isaac imitated both the good and the bad that he saw in his dad.

So, are we doomed to follow the sinful and destructive patterns, attitudes, and actions passed down from our parents and grandparents?

CHAPTER 2

NOT NECESSARILY

Doomed is probably too strong a word to use, but the fact remains - our lives are greatly impacted by the physical, emotional, and spiritual choices and behaviors of our ancestors - as are the lives of our children and grandchildren affected by ours.

Even though my beloved sister-in-law is fond of saying, "Why mess up a good story with facts", the following facts are not only sobering but also help to make a point.

According to a 2017 research study of over 3 million children, led by Sytske Besemer at the University of California Berkeley -

- Children of criminal parents are nearly 2 to 3 times more likely to exhibit criminal behavior and fall into crime than children of non-criminal parents.

According to the American Academy of Child and Adolescent Psychiatry -

- Alcoholism runs in families, and children of alcoholics are 4 times more likely than children from non-alcoholic parents to become alcoholics themselves.

In 2019, after conducting twenty-five studies into child behavior, this same American Academy of Child and Adolescent Psychiatry found that children were significantly more likely to have anxiety and depressive disorders if their parents had anxiety disorders. They concluded that children whose parents have anxiety disorders are 2 to 7 times more likely to develop similar disorders. Sadly, recent figures show that nearly 31% of American adults suffer from one or more anxiety disorders (National Center for Complementary and Integrative Health).

Also worthy of mentioning is a 2021 research study of over 1 million young people conducted in Wales that found -

- Children born to mothers suffering from depression, or who live with a mother who suffers from depression, are up to 75% more likely to suffer depression than those whose mother does not.

Research done by the National Center for Health Statistics concluded that over 41% of American adults report struggling with depressive and anxiety disorders.

That means that nearly half the people we interact with on a daily basis - our family, friends, colleagues, and strangers have struggled or are currently struggling with anxiety and/or depression. When coupled with the research results mentioned earlier, it is not hard to see that there are millions of people whose lives have been profoundly and negatively impacted by the physical and emotional influences of their parents...and those parents were likewise impacted by their parents.

These powerful influences impact both Christian children and non-Christian. Just because a grandparent, parent, or young person is a born-again Christian doesn't insulate them from being visited by those unwanted hand-me-downs.

In my own family line, and that of my wife, we can identify many such negative generational influences:

Alcoholism
Addiction
Anger
Adultery
Divorce
Insecurity
Materialism
Passivity / Indecisiveness
Pride

Thankfully, we can also identify:
Professing, Devoted Christians
Pastors, Church leaders
Successful, Hardworking Businessmen/Athletic
Sense of Humor
Steadfast - Patient
Maritally faithful

A couple of significant Bible passages to know regarding this issue are:

Keeping mercy for thousands, forgiving iniquity and transgression and sin, and that will by no means clear the guilty; visiting the iniquity of the fathers upon the children, and upon the children's children, unto the third and to the fourth generations. **Exodus 34:7 KJV**

The soul that sinneth, it shall die. The son shall not bear the iniquity of the father, neither shall the father bear the iniquity of the son: the righteousness of the righteous shall be upon him, and the wickedness of the wicked shall be upon him. **Ezekiel 18:17 KJV**

The word "iniquity" means to have "a bent or propensity toward a certain behavior". If you have ever traveled along the Gulf Coast of Alabama, Louisiana, Mississippi, and Florida, you can't help but notice the rugged oak trees that exhibit a significant leaning away from the beach. These trees are considered the most hurricane-resistant trees in America, but even the mighty oaks show the obvious effects of regularly resisting the impact of hurricane-force winds.

Generational iniquities create *winds* that blow against us and the effects become more noticeable as the years pass on. Thankfully, God does not punish us for our predecessors' iniquities and sins, but He allows these *winds* of iniquity to blow in order to remind us of our dependency on Him and also to remind us that, in Him, we have the power and authority to overcome them in our lives and also in the lives of the generations that follow.

All of us are affected by the *winds* (choices, habits, addictions, mistakes, successes, decisions, lifestyles, words, temperament, and affections) of our parents, grandparents, and great-grandparents. The good ones and the bad ones. We all will carry the "bent" from our family tree. Sadly, many Christians accept their wind-blown status as "just the way I am", or "the way our family is". They concede in their soul that they will never be able to stand straight, tall, and free like other "trees", and accept a powerless, struggle-prone, and joyless Christian life.

My fellow *trees* - God wants to convince us otherwise:

- *He has sent me to proclaim freedom to the captives and recovery of sight to the blind, to set the oppressed free.* **Luke 4:18**

- *If you abide in my word, you are truly my disciples, and you will know the truth, and the truth will set you free.* **John 8:31-32**

- *For the law of the Spirit of life has set you free in Christ Jesus from the law of sin and death.* **Romans 8:2**

- *So if the Son sets you free, you will be free indeed.* **John 8:36**

- *I have come that you might have life, and have it abundantly.* **John 10:10**

- *For sin will have no dominion over you, since you are not under law but under grace.* **Romans 6:14**

- *It is for freedom that Christ has set us free. Stand firm then, and do not let yourselves be burdened again by a yoke of slavery.* **Galatians 5:1**

- *Live as people who are free.* **1 Peter 2:16**

It is obvious that God desires all of His children to walk in freedom and be released from the burden of personal sin and generational iniquity. So much so, that He sent His only Son, Jesus, to earth, to suffer a gruesome, painful death to offer his blood to cancel the curse of sin once and for all - for us.

This day I call the heavens and the earth as witnesses against you that I have set before you life and death, blessings and curses. Now choose life, so that you and your children may live and that you may love the Lord your God, listen to his voice, and hold fast to him.

Deuteronomy 30:19-20a

CHAPTER 3

NOTHING BUT THE BLOOD

We are all impacted greatly by the positive and negative behaviors and choices of our ancestors before us. But, there is one ancestor who we have been most affected by - because his actions alone placed every human being born afterward under a curse - the curse of sin and death. Let's take a minute to refresh our memory regarding curses and blood in the time after Adam's sin....

After Adam and Eve sinned in the Garden of Eden, God had to sacrifice (shed the blood of) animals in order to "fashion clothing" to cover them both. (**Genesis 3:21**). This shedding of blood served to counteract the curse that would have otherwise come upon them personally for their sin....stay with me here.

God cursed the serpent (Satan), and the ground (work) mankind would eat from (make a living). He did not, however, curse Adam and Eve because there was "the shedding of blood", but their offspring would be forever born under this curse- unless it was broken by the future shedding of blood According to the Law of God, and the Old Testament covenant - blood represented life. Because of this, God chose to use a blood sacrifice as part of the sacrificial system of the

Jewish people. Each time blood was shed, it reminded the people of life and death, sin and forgiveness.

For the life of a creature is in the blood, and I have given it to you to make atonement for yourselves on the altar; it is the blood that makes atonement for one's life. **Leviticus 17:11**

Without the shedding of blood, there is no forgiveness for sin. **Hebrews 9:22b**

Beginning with the sons of Adam and Eve, the Bible is filled with story after story of blood sacrifices being offered to God for the forgiveness of His people's sins.

Then Noah built an altar to the Lord, and took some of every kind of clean animal and some of every clean bird and offered burnt offerings on the altar. **Genesis 8:20**

Some time later God tested Abraham. He said to him, "Abraham!" "Here I am," he replied. Then God said, "Take your son, your only son, whom you love—Isaac—and go to the region of Moriah. Sacrifice him there as a burnt offering on a mountain I will show you."

Early the next morning Abraham got up and loaded his donkey. He took with him two of his servants and his son Isaac. When he had cut enough wood for the burnt offering, he set out for the place God had told him about. On the third day, Abraham looked up and saw the place in the distance. He said to his servants, "Stay here with the donkey while I and the boy go over there. We will worship and then we will come back to you."

Abraham took the wood for the burnt offering and placed it on his son Isaac, and he himself carried the fire and the knife. As the two of them went on together, Isaac spoke up and said to his father Abraham, "Father?" "Yes, my son?" Abraham replied.

"The fire and wood are here," Isaac said, *"but where is the lamb for the burnt offering?"* Abraham answered, *"God himself will provide the lamb for the burnt offering, my son."* And the two of them went on together.

When they reached the place God had told him about, Abraham built an altar there and arranged the wood on it. He bound his son Isaac and laid him on the altar, on top of the wood. Then he reached out his hand and took the knife to slay his son. But the angel of the Lord called out to him from heaven, *"Abraham! Abraham!"* *"Here I am,"* he replied. *"Do not lay a hand on the boy,"* he said. *"Do not do anything to him. Now I know that you fear God because you have not withheld from me your son, your only son."*

Abraham looked up and there in a thicket, he saw a ram caught by its horns. He went over and took the ram and sacrificed it as a burnt offering instead of his son. So Abraham called that place The Lord Will Provide. And to this day it is said, *"On the mountain of the Lord it will be provided."*
Genesis 22:1-14

Then Moses summoned all the elders of Israel and said to them, "Go at once and select the animals for your families and slaughter the Passover lamb. Take a bunch of hyssop, dip it into the blood in the basin, and put some of the blood on the top and on both sides of the doorframe. None of you shall go out of the door of your house until morning. When the Lord goes through the land to strike down the Egyptians, he will see the blood on the top and sides of the doorframe and will pass over that doorway, and he will not permit the destroyer to enter your houses and strike you down.

"Obey these instructions as a lasting ordinance for you and your descendants. When you enter the land that the Lord will give you as he promised, observe this ceremony. And when your children ask you, 'What does this ceremony mean to you?' then tell them, 'It is the Passover sacrifice to the Lord, who passed over the houses of the Israelites in Egypt and spared our homes when he struck down the Egyptians.'" Then the people bowed down

and worshiped. The Israelites did just what the Lord commanded Moses and Aaron. **Exodus 12:21-28**

"Aaron shall bring the bull for his own sin offering to make atonement for himself and his household, and he is to slaughter the bull for his own sin offering. He is to take a censer full of burning coals from the altar before the Lord and two handfuls of finely ground fragrant incense and take them behind the curtain. He is to put the incense on the fire before the Lord, and the smoke of the incense will conceal the atonement cover above the tablets of the covenant law so that he will not die. He is to take some of the bull's blood and with his finger sprinkle it on the front of the atonement cover; then he shall sprinkle some of it with his finger seven times before the atonement cover.

"He shall then slaughter the goat for the sin offering for the people and take its blood behind the curtain and do with it as he did with the bull's blood: He shall sprinkle it on the atonement cover and in front of it. In this way, he will make atonement for the Most Holy Place because of the uncleanness and rebellion of the Israelites, whatever their sins have been. He is to do the same for the tent of meeting, which is among them in the midst of their uncleanness. No one is to be in the tent of meeting from the time Aaron goes in to make atonement in the Most Holy Place until he comes out, having made atonement for himself, his household, and the whole community of Israel.

"Then he shall come out to the altar that is before the Lord and make atonement for it. He shall take some of the bull's *blood and some of the goat's blood and put it on all the horns of the altar. He shall sprinkle some of the blood on it with his finger seven times to cleanse it and to consecrate it from the uncleanness of the Israelites.* **Leviticus 16:11-19**

These a just a sampling of the examples of Old Covenant saints making blood sacrifices for the forgiveness/atonement of their sins.

The most holy Day of Atonement ceremony was performed by the High Priest alone, and animals were sacrificed as a sin offering for the sins of the priest and for the sins of the people. Sin Offerings were offered to wash away the guilt for sin and bring forgiveness (**Leviticus 4:1-12**).

What we need to understand today, is that anyone who has yet to receive Jesus' sacrificial death (blood) on the cross on their behalf as the payment (forgiveness/atonement) for their sin, is still under that curse of sin and death passed down from Adam. No amount of counseling, self-control, self-help, positive thinking, good works, medication, or wishful thinking will ever be powerful enough to shield them from the curse of sin they received from their ancient ancestors - or keep them from further passing them on to their children. Worse yet - they are choosing an eternity apart from God.

In the same way that the blood of a lamb protected the people of Israel from the angel of death in Egypt, only the blood of Jesus will cover us and protect us from the original curse of sin/death passed down from Adam.

But if we walk in the light, as he is in the light, we have fellowship with one another, and the blood of Jesus, his Son, purifies us from all sin.
1 John 1:7
In him we have redemption through his blood, the forgiveness of our sins. **Ephesians 1:7**
But now, in Christ Jesus, you who were once far off have been brought near by the blood of Christ. **Ephesians 2:13**
For He made Him who knew no sin to be sin for us, that we might become the righteousness of God in Him. **2 Corinthians 5:21**

Christ and Christ Crucified

The wages of my sin was death
You knew I couldn't pay the debt
You paid it with Your final breath
Oh hallelujah hallelujah

You took the wrath that I deserved
Your holy blood broke every curse
Your mercy had the final word
Oh hallelujah hallelujah

We sing Christ and Christ
Crucified In You
We're raised from death to life
We sing Christ and Christ crucified
Hallelujah hallelujah

Circuit Rider Music

So the bottom line is this - Christians have been freed from the original and eternal curse of sin and death brought upon the human race by the sin/disobedience of Adam. We are no longer under the curse but we do live in a fallen, sinful world and face a relentless assault from the enemy of God who is hell-bent on "devouring" us (1 Peter 5:8) and everyone we hold dear.

We are also not bound to live under any iniquities, failures or curses passed down to us from our parents or other ancestors. Make no mistake - they will be "visited" upon us, meaning we may have a strong, natural propensity toward them - but, with the discernment of the Holy Spirit and the power and authority we have in Jesus' name - we can defeat their influence over us and our heritage.

BUT - before we dive into the deep water, we have to settle one thing...the MAIN thing.

"The main thing
is to keep the main thing
the main thing."

~ Stephen Covey

CHAPTER 4

THE MAIN THING

As a teen, I knew that becoming a Christian assured me of an eternity in heaven. I knew I needed to read my Bible, go to church, and pray. Beyond that, I was amazingly naive regarding "who" I actually became the moment I believed. Because of that, I lived far too many years in struggle and defeat. Somewhere along the way, I missed the key to the abundant life, the life of victory and freedom - I missed the MAIN THING.

There are dozens of fundamental truths believers in Christ must know (in their heads) and believe (in their hearts) if we are going to be able to "wrestle against principalities, powers, and spiritual wickedness" (**Ephesians 6:12**) and win - and to finally break free from the generational sin patterns that Satan uses to "kill, steal, destroy" us (**John 10:10**).

It is my opinion that one of the most significant of these truths falls under the heading of knowing - Who I really am in Christ. Unless and until a believer truly knows, embraces, and lives in the power of this truth, he or she will never be able to experience the abundant life and freedom promised by Jesus.

The following list is by no means exhaustive, but I think you will get the idea. My prayer is that you will not only look up these verses in your Bible and get familiar with them but that you will literally begin to profess (out loud) these verses whenever you begin to recognize the enemy's lies, innuendos, deceptions, and accusations. You and I have been given:

- The armor of God to protect us (**Ephesians 6**)
- Divinely powerful weapons to pull down strongholds (**2 Corinthians 10:4**)
- The authority of God to wield these weapons (**Luke 10:17-20**).....

but, all of these are useless if we don't know we have them and learn how to use them. We have all the tools we need to break free from generational iniquity and from "all the power of the evil one".

<u>The only power the enemy has over us is the power we allow him to have.</u>

Take a minute and look back at the last sentence, and let it sink in.... you and I give Satan permission to exercise power over us!

Now - on to the list of truths we should immediately begin to walk in and profess in battle. This, my brother or sister, is who you REALLY are as a believer in Jesus. It is who God created you to be, and how He wants you to live.

- I am greatly loved by God (John 3:16; John 15:9, Ephesians 1:4-5, Ephesians 2:1-5 and 3:19).

- I am chosen by God (John 15:16, 2 Thessalonians 2:13, Ephesians 1:4, 2:4-5 and 3:12, 1 Peter 2:9).

- I am a child of God (John 1:12-13, Romans 8:14-16, 2 Corinthians 6:18, Galatians 3:26 and 4:7, Ephesians1:4-5, Hebrews 2:11).

- I am bought with a price and have great value (1 Corinthians 6:20).

- I am Jesus' friend (John 15:15)

- God is always with me and will never leave me (Hebrews 13:5-6, John 14:16, Matthew 28:20).

- I am a joint heir with Jesus (Romans 8:16-17, Galatians 3:29 and 4:7, 1 Peter 1:4, Titus 3:7).

- My citizenship is in heaven and I'm a member of God's household (Philippians 3:18-20).

- I am Christ's ambassador, and a light in the world (2 Corinthians 5:20, Matthew 5:14).

- I am assured of eternal life (John 3:16, 1 John 5:11, Romans 6:23 and 8:38-39).

- I am seated with Christ in heavenly places, far above all rule and authority, power and dominion (Ephesians 2).

- Jesus rescued me from the domain and the power of darkness and brought me into God's kingdom (Colossians 1:13).

- I am a new creation. I have been given a new nature and am no longer a slave to sin (2 Corinthians 5:17, Ephesians 4:24, Colossians 3:9, Romans 6:18 and 8:2, Galatians 5:24).

- I am completely and forever forgiven of my past, present, and future sins (Psalm 103:12, Isaiah 43:25, Ephesians 1:7, 1 John 1:9, Hebrews 8:12).

- I am forever free from any condemnation for my sin (Romans 8:1, Psalm 34:22, John 3:18).

- I am holy and without blame before Him in love (Ephesians 1:4; 2 Corinthians 5:21, Colossians 3:3, 12)

- I have been made the righteousness of God and my life is hidden in Christ (2 Corinthians 5:21, Colossians 3:3)

- I am no longer considered a sinner but a saint (Ephesians 1:1)

- The Spirit of God (and all of His power) lives in me. I am His temple (1 John 4:4, Ephesians 1:15-23, 1 Corinthians 3:16).

- I can approach God anytime and anywhere with complete confidence and freedom as His beloved child (Ephesians 3:12).

- I can do whatever I need to do in life through Christ Jesus who gives me strength (Philippians 4:13).

- God is working everything that happens to me in life together for my good (Romans 8:28)

- God supplies all of my needs according to His riches in glory in Christ Jesus (Philippians 4:19).

- I have everything I need to live a godly life and am equipped to live in His divine nature (2 Peter 1:3-4).

- I am God's workmanship, created in Christ to do good works that He has prepared for me to do (Ephesians 2:10).

- I have been commissioned by Jesus to engage and defeat the enemy (Matthew 16:18, Mark 16:17-18, Luke 17-20, Ephesians 1:19-23).

- God has given me "divinely powerful" weapons to defeat the enemy (2 Corinthians 10:3-4).

- God has given me authority (in Jesus) to use these weapons (Luke 10:19).

- If I resist the devil or his demons, they will flee from me (James 4:7).

- I have the authority to invoke Jesus' name to defeat the enemy (Mark 16:14-18, Luke 10:17, Acts 3:1-6 and 16).

And these are just the tip of the iceberg. Many more truths are "hidden in plain sight" in God's Word, and that is precisely why we should be saturating our minds with it daily, and wielding it in spiritual battles (see **Ephesians 6:17, Hebrews 4:12, Romans 1:16**). If we ever hope to live a life free from habitual sin and any sinful, hand-me-down influences of our ancestors, we have to know who we are in Christ and what His Word says about us.

Look at this profound example from **Matthew 4:1-6**:

Then Jesus was led by the Spirit into the wilderness to be tempted by the devil. After fasting forty days and forty nights, he was hungry. The tempter came to him and said, "If you are the Son of God, tell these stones to become bread." Jesus answered, "It is written: 'Man shall not live by bread alone, but on every word that comes from the mouth of God.'"

Then the devil took him to the holy city and had him stand on the highest point of the temple. "If you are the Son of God," he said, "throw yourself down. For it is written: "He will command his angels concerning you, and they will lift you up in their hands, so that you will not strike your foot against a stone."

Did you catch that?

Satan's first two temptations of Jesus himself, were begun with the words - "If you are the Son of God". Satan was questioning whether Jesus was who he said he was (his identity) and may have been trying to cause Jesus to even doubt it himself. Thankfully, Jesus knew exactly who he was and immediately let Satan know it. Interestingly, Satan even quotes Scripture in his second temptation, and Jesus trumps his scripture with a scripture of his own.

Remember how Satan manipulated God's Word to Eve in a manner intended to make her question God and doubt His goodness? Check this out.....

Now the serpent was more crafty than any of the wild animals the Lord God had made. He said to the woman, "Did God really say, 'You must not eat from any tree in the garden'?" **Genesis 3:1**

The reason believers are told repeatedly that we need to "read, study and meditate on God's Word" is not because "that's what good Christian boys and girls should do", but because it is critical that we know what God says so we are not deceived by Satan's clever lies and schemes. Knowing His Word is not optional for the Christian who wishes to walk in freedom and victory. His Word is our primary offensive weapon as we battle the enemy. **Ephesians 6:17**

So Jesus said to the Jews who had believed him, "If you abide in my word, you are truly my disciples, and you will know the truth, and the truth will set you free." **John 8:31-32**

For the word of God is alive and active. Sharper than any double-edged sword, it penetrates even to dividing soul and spirit, joints and marrow; it judges the thoughts and attitudes of the heart. **Hebrews 4:12**

Knowing what God says about you is one of the most crucial pillars of your Christian foundation. Without knowing it, we are sitting ducks for our mortal enemy, whose primary goal in life is to - *kill, steal, and destroy* the lives of believers (**John 10:10**). Knowing it gives us the most powerful, offensive weapon we need to be victorious in the ongoing battle against the forces of darkness.

When we hear Satan's accusing voice/thought in our mind saying - "you are a failure", "you will never amount to anything", or "God can't use someone like you", "You're a loser" etc., etc. - we need to learn to imitate what Jesus did when he was tempted by the devil. Without hesitation, he reminded Satan of the truth of God's Word and told him to "depart from me". (Note: Eve, on the other hand, began to ponder Satan's words and was completely deceived and defeated).

From the list in the early part of the chapter, see if you can find a corresponding truth that dispels a few sample lies, like:

- No one could love me (example) * I am greatly loved - John 3:16
- God surely couldn't forgive what I have done
- I am worthless. I'm no use to God
- I'll never change. I'll always be like this.
- God doesn't care about what I'm going through

- I'm such a failure as a husband/wife
- Am I even a Christian

I hope you will start to see what a huge difference knowing and standing on God's Word makes in winning the battles for your soul. Satan still uses that tactic he used on Jesus very effectively against Christians every day. If he can cause us to doubt our true identity, and keep us believing that we are just "sinners saved by grace", instead of royalty (as God's children), joint heirs with Jesus, filled with the all-powerful Holy Spirit of God and given "mighty weapons by God and the authority of use them - he can keep us in chains, powerless, joyless, and impotent as we wrestle the "principalities and powers" that assault us and those we love.

So, the main thing is this - to commit the time and energy to stay immersed in God's Word, and know what He says about you as His beloved son or daughter. No more hiding behind the term "quiet time". That has become Christian code for "I read my five-minute devotional", or a brief Bible passage and checked "read my Bible" off my "good Christian boy/girl list - so, now I can go about my life and do what I need to do today".

God's Word is not an app we access when a need arises. His truth is oxygen. It is nourishment. It is vital. It is our primary offensive weapon in spiritual warfare.

It is:
- our sword (Ephesians 6:17)
- our guide (Psalm 119:105, 130)
- our protection (Psalm 119:11)
- our source of faith (Romans 10:17)
- our teacher and correction (2 Timothy 3:16-17)

- our stability (Psalm 119:165)
- our assurance of success (Joshua 1:8) (Luke 11:28)
- our God, Himself (John 1:1)

We have one offensive weapon: the sword of the Spirit, the Word of God (Eph. 6:17). But what many Christians fail to realize is that we can't draw the sword from someone else's scabbard. If we don't wear it, we can't wield it. If the Word of God does not abide in us (Jn. 15:7), we will reach for it in vain when the enemy strikes. But if we do wear it, if it lives within us, what mighty warriors we can be. ~John Piper

CHAPTER 5

SOUND FAMILIAR

O Sovereign Lord! You made the heavens and earth by your strong hand and powerful arm. Nothing is too hard for you!

You show unfailing love to thousands, but you also bring the consequences of one generation's sin upon the next. You are the great and powerful God, the Lord of Heaven's Armies.

You have all wisdom and do great and mighty miracles. You see the conduct of all people, and you give them what they deserve.

Jeremiah 32:17-19

This powerful passage is both encouraging and frightening. "Nothing is too hard for the Lord" - "You show unfailing love to thousands" - "You are great and powerful" - and "You have all wisdom and perform mighty miracles" - what great verses to know, to memorize, to quote regularly! But, we can't overlook the equally powerful, yet sobering, admonitions to God's people (us).....

"You also bring the consequences of one generation's sin upon the next"

Similar to Exodus 34, this verse reminds us that our ancestors' sinful choices impact us spiritually, emotionally, and even physically unless and until they are dealt with.

Think about this - in the 12 generations before you were born, there were some 4096 people involved. Obviously, the number doubles when considering both you and your spouse. So, in the last 36oish years, any one or more of them could have been involved with the occult, astrology, witchcraft, crime, adultery, mental illness, and more. The opposite could also be true. You could have ancestors who were committed Christians, pastors, lay leaders, prayer warriors, community leaders, athletes, entrepreneurs and financially successful.

Is it too hard to imagine that some might have suffered from abuse, depression, insecurity, anxiety, or anger issues - while others enjoyed great emotional stability? Were any of yours addicts, alcoholics, promiscuous, adulterers, gluttons, perfectionists, controlling?

Most of us, myself included, never think much about it. It is extremely important to go back as many generations as you can, to discover as many possible patterns/wounds/tendencies/behaviors as you possibly can, in order to address them and get rid of their influence over you and all future generations.

I don't remember much from Biology class, but I do remember studying about parasites. Certain types of these creatures invade a human host and cause all types of symptoms and even diseases. The host is usually oblivious to their existence until the arrival of symptoms. These can range from very mild to quite severe.

So, am I saying your relatives were parasites? No, but I hope the illustration serves to shine a bit of light on the reality that we are affected greatly by the generational sins/choices of our parents, their parents, their parents, etc. These effects can often be seen in young children, but most often "lay dormant" until surfacing later in life - as teenagers, when we get married, while we're raising our children, or sustaining a enjoyable, long-term marriage.

Have you ever wondered, "why did I react like that?", or "why did that bother me so much?" after a confrontation with your boss, spouse, or child? Most of us have entertained thoughts like, 'why can't I get over this?', 'why am I so worried' or "why can't I quit doing this?'

Have you ever noticed your child acting "just like his father or mother", or heard someone say, "she's just like her mother", or "he's his father's son" referring to the child's behavior? The saying, "the apple doesn't fall far from the tree" has been referring to this truism for decades.

I can come up with far too many examples from my own life, but a few that come to mind are:
- realizing I had an inner inclination toward alcohol even as a pre-teen
- realizing how insecure I was when entering middle school
- realizing how selfish I was while living with college roommates
- realizing even more so how selfish I was after getting married
- my wife and I realizing that divorce "ran in our families" and vowing never to consider that an option
- realizing alcoholism ran in both our families and that we were slowly being drawn in that direction

The list really is longer than I like to admit, but the point is - we ALL have a list, and it is most likely longer than you think too.

Let me throw out a few "symptoms" for you to ponder and, better yet, talk with the Lord about. He may add a few you haven't thought of.

If you are brutally honest with yourself, would you say you have exhibited any of these in the past or even at present? Have you seen or experienced any of these in your mother or father? Grandparents?.....

Depression/Suicide
Anxiety/Panic attacks
Fear
Insecurity
Negativity/Judgemental
Indecision/ Avoidance
Immorality/Promiscuity/Flirtation
Adultery
Addiction (alcohol, drugs, gambling, sexual, etc.)
Idolatry
Pride
Selfishness
Compromise
Negativity/Cynicism
Anger/Violent behavior
Abuse (emotional, physical, sexual, verbal)
Hatred/Cruelty
Prejudice/Racism
Unforgiveness/Bitterness
Divorce
Mental illness
Chronic Physical illness/Premature death
Materialism/Greed
Workaholism
Perfectionism

Poverty
Chronic financial or work hardship
Laziness/Apathy/Victimhood
Codependency
Spendthrift
Controlling
Manipulation/Narcissism/Entitlement
Disrespect (parents, authority, others)
Dishonoring parents
Dishonesty
Rebellion
Lying/Deception
Unbelief
Obesity/Eating disorders
Religious or Legalistic spirit

Do any others come to mind?

_____
_____
_____
_____
_____
_____

When you identify which ones you feel may be influencing your spiritual, emotional, or physical life, or your attitudes and behaviors today, it is time to get down to business.

But, before you begin we must discuss a couple of crucial points:

1. The authority and power to break free from the cycle of generational iniquity is only available to God's children. If you don't consider yourself a born-again Christian (a follower of Jesus) please take a few minutes to read and consider **Appendix A** in the back of the book.

The Bible is clear that because of the original sin, committed by the original couple (see **Genesis 2:16-17 and 3**), mankind has lived under a curse. The Bible calls this "the curse of sin", which is basically a life apart from the benevolence and protection of God (which was mankind's original relationship), and slogging our way through a life of struggle, heartache, death, and then, eternal death.

This life apart from the love and mercy of God is what sets the stage for the broken lives and lifestyles that our ancestors lived and "visited" upon us. As Christians, however, we have been "redeemed from the curse of sin and death" and transferred back to the kingdom of God where we were originally meant to be.

Since generational iniquities/sins come through bloodlines, they can only be canceled and removed by blood. Jesus' shed blood on the cross paid the penalty for our sin and broke the curse over us once and for all. The Bible is clear that anyone not covered by Jesus' redemption is still under the curse of sin, dysfunction, and death. Appendix A will go into greater detail for you if needed.

Christ redeemed us from the curse of the law by becoming a curse for us, for it is written: "Cursed is everyone who is hung on a tree." **Galatians 3:13-14**

For as in Adam all died, so also in Christ shall all be made alive. **1 Corinthians 15:22**

For all have sinned and fall short of the glory of God, and all are justified freely by his grace through the redemption that came by Christ Jesus. God presented Christ as a sacrifice of atonement, through the shedding of his blood—to be received by faith. He did this to demonstrate his righteousness because in his forbearance he had left the sins committed beforehand unpunished. **Romans 3:23-25**

Therefore, as one trespass led to condemnation for all men, so one act of righteousness leads to justification and life for all men. **Romans 5:18**

2. Secondly, you may logically be asking - "Are all my "issues" the result of having received hand-me-downs from my ancestors?" While many are, the answer would have to be "no" to the question "are ALL". While their lifestyle choices, toxic habits, crippling words, actions, and emotions may be part of your inheritance, you are not automatically bound to repeat them. They may be "visited upon" you, but you don't have to put them on and wear them. Thankfully, we get to make choices.

As far back as I can remember, my father drank beer. As a professional baseball player, drinking after a game was just standard practice. But he also drank on days off and after he quit playing altogether. And he drank quite a bit. My first taste of beer was as a batboy after one of his games. I was tasked with fetching players whatever brand of ice-cold brew they desired out of the long, ice-filled coolers. I was captivated by baseball, baseball players, and baseball cards - and, was only in elementary school. As the curious young hoodlum I was, I began occasionally taking the liberty of sneaking a sip or two (or three) from the bottles I was delivering. Sadly, I really liked the taste of beer.

My dad also smoked. He was what is called a "chain smoker", even though he was a tremendous athlete, he, like his father before him (and his father before him), would light up one cigarette after another. I am taken back to my childhood every time I smell cigarette smoke. Smoking, like alcohol (beer), was "visited upon me" - but I hated it. One puff and I was repulsed for life. I just couldn't understand how someone could do such a thing to themselves.

Both iniquities (habits, tendencies, leanings) were heavily present in my family line. Both were visited upon me. I didn't automatically, robotically comply with accepting them and making them a part of my life - I got to choose. We always get to choose. Just because my wife and I come from divorced, alcoholic, adulterous families, doesn't mean we are automatically doomed to repeat that life or pass those tendencies, and the damage thereof, down to our children.

Once again, the Bible provides us with real-life stories on this subject. No matter what may be visited upon us (good or evil), our life choices are still ours to make.

A more dedicated and righteous prophet and judge than Samuel is not seen in the Bible and, yet, Samuel had two of the most wicked sons in Joel and Abijah.

Mannasseh was one of the most wicked men mentioned in the Bible and, yet, his father was the godly Hezekiah, who the Bible says, "did what was right in the eyes of the Lord "just as his father David had done".

In contrast, consider the lives of:

Josiah - stands out in Bible history as one of the most eminent kings of Judah despite both his father (Amon) and grandfather being exceedingly wicked.

King Hezekiah was the godly son of his evil father, Ahaz, who the Bible says, "Unlike David his father, he did not do what was right in the eyes of the Lord his God.

So, godly parents can walk with God and still have a child or children who make decisions counter to the beliefs and training they received from them. Wicked, dysfunctional parents can raise kids whose choices break them free from the sinful patterns and curses they were born into.

Here is a modern-day story to that point....

Ben Carson was born on the southwest side of Detroit, Michigan to a mother who could not read. He spent much of his youth in what he has described as "dire poverty," depending heavily on government assistance. Called "dummy" by his middle school classmates, until his mother, a housekeeper, made him stay inside to read instead of going outside to play, and then turn in book reports to her on what he had read. Within a year, he was making the best grades in class and his classmates started asking him for help.

Mrs. Carson was a single mom, married at 13 and with a 3rd-grade education, struggling to raise two sons on a maid's wages. She worked two and sometimes three jobs to keep food on the table for her family. Occasionally the pressures would overtake her and she would have to "be away" for psychiatric treatment. In his book,

Gifted Hands, he says of his mother, "She cleaned other people's houses, but she never developed a victim mentality and she didn't let her kids develop one either."

Thus began Ben Carson's life of accomplishment - reaching the highest rank in junior ROTC in high school, a full scholarship to Yale, graduating from the University of Michigan Medical School, and eventually becoming chief of pediatric neurosurgery at Johns Hopkins Children's Center in Baltimore - and the 17th U.S. Secretary of Housing and Urban Development from 2017-2021. Raised in poverty, in a broken home, from the ghetto, dependent on the government, being repeatedly told he was stupid, with his mom's psychiatric issues and his father's issues as well.... the cards were all stacked against Ben Carson.

Poverty, divorce, verbal abuse from peers, family mental issues, absent father, low self-esteem, and probably much more were "visited upon" him. So, why didn't he automatically turn out the same as his parents? With the encouragement of his mother, he began to make choices. As he began to see the fruit of his choice to heed his mother's advice and bear down on his reading and studies, he began to see progress. His grades improved and even jumped ahead of his teasing classmates. His self-esteem flourished and his entire view of the world and his future also changed. He began to want to be a doctor and had a new belief that he might actually be able to achieve that.

His choices to work harder than he had ever worked paid great dividends. Not only did he become a doctor, but he became a world-renowned one. Divorce and a broken family were not options for Dr. Carson and his wife of now 49 years, Candy. His three sons have also found success in their own right.

Carson's oldest, Rhoeyce, graduated from the University of Delaware in 2008 and went on to attend Stevenson University from 2008 until 2011. He is currently an associate at Clifton, Larson, Allen in Baltimore, the 10th-largest accountancy firm in the United States.

Carson's second son, Ben, Jr. studied at Tufts University from 2003 to 2007 and earned a Bachelor of Arts in Entrepreneurial Leadership. He serves on the Board of Directors for the Carson Scholars Fund, Inc., and is Chairman of ARGO Systems, LLC and Co-Founder of Fvlcrum Funds.

Murray Carson, the youngest, is a graduate of Yale University with a BS in Mechanical Engineering and earned a Master's of Science in Applied Information Technology from Towson University. He also speaks fluent Spanish. Murray worked as a mechanical engineer at Lockheed Martin as well as Director of Software Solutions for Restyn. He is currently working as CRM Technologist for Adventist Information Ministry.

Needless to say, the choices Ben Carson made to get serious about his grades through reading books and to actually study his lessons (with the encouragement of his mother) have paid huge dividends in the lives of his sons. No one in the family has been called "dummy" at school, forced to live in poverty, take low-paying jobs, or suffer from low self-esteem as a result of Carson's family history.

He and Candy have risen above the life circumstances they were dealt by making difficult but powerful choices. The biggest choice was for each to give their lives to Jesus and allow His blood on the cross to cover and break the family curses from previous generations.

Thanks to Adam, we are all born into a sinful world as sinners, spiritually dead and separated from God.

As for you, <u>you were dead in your transgressions and sins</u>, in which you used to live when <u>you followed the ways of this world and of the ruler of the kingdom of the air, the spirit who is now at work in those who are disobedient</u>. All of us also <u>lived among them at one time, gratifying the cravings of our flesh and following its desires and thoughts</u>. Like the rest, <u>we were by nature deserving of wrath</u>. But because of his great love for us, God, who is rich in mercy, made us alive with Christ even when <u>we were dead in transgressions</u>—it is by grace you have been saved. **Ephesians 2:1-5**

Did you catch all that? We were born "dead" in our sin; followed the ruler (Satan) of this world; disobedient, satisfying our own fleshly thoughts and cravings. We deserved God's wrath (eternal punishment) from birth.

So I tell you this, and insist on it in the Lord, that you must no longer live as the Gentiles do, in the <u>futility of their thinking</u>. They are <u>darkened in their understanding</u> and <u>separated from the life of God</u> because of the ignorance that is in them due to the <u>hardening of their hearts</u>. Having lost all sensitivity, they have <u>given themselves over to sensuality</u> so as to indulge in every kind of impurity, and they are <u>full of greed</u>. **Ephesians 4:17-19**

Our original state was that of futility, darkened understanding, separated from God, with hearts that were hardened to the things of God, given to sensuality, and full of selfish greed.

Ephesians 2;11-12 reminds us that we were also. "without Christ, strangers to the promises of God, having no hope and without God in this world".

Psalm 51:5 tells us, we were brought forth in iniquity, and born in sin.

2 Corinthians 4:4 states that we were blinded by Satan to the truths of God's gospel.

Romans 5:12 tells us that death (separation from God) spread to all of us from the original sin of Adam.

The sad truth is - all of us are born sinners, separated from God, without hope, and lost as we can be. We must first recognize and deal with our own sin, and choose to accept or reject Christ's sacrificial atonement for those sins.

No matter what our decision is, we will still be impacted by both good and bad traits, mindsets, choices, lifestyles, and habits of our ancestors. We will also be influenced by their words and any trauma inflicted on them or by them.

Because of this, we all have one or more closets in our souls, full of hand-me-downs from our ancestors. One of the hardest but most beneficial things we can do in life is take the time to sort through those closets and decide what to throw out. We will no doubt find good things in there - joyful things, beneficial, positive things, and multitudes of blessings. But we cannot turn a blind eye to the painful, debilitating, and sometimes even evil contents we may find.

While we rejoice in the blessings received from our relatives, we have to learn how to finally deal with the tendencies, habits, behaviors, bents, and curses we discover.

Time to open the closet ...

It's up to us to break generational curses
when they say "it runs in the family"
you tell them "this is where it runs out".

The Minds Journal

CHAPTER 6

DISCOVERY

Okay. It's time to make YOUR list. You have most likely already identified with one or more of the emotional and behavioral iniquities I mentioned in earlier chapters. As you read the descriptions, ie: addiction, depression, anxiety, divorce, etc. - something inside you said "yes", or maybe you felt a tinge of agreement, guilt, or conviction.

Start your list with those that are most glaring and obvious to you personally. Even though you may discover some generational patterns of behavior that have been handed down to you, you are still responsible for wearing them. Ask yourself a very honest question.......

"What are the behavioral patterns, habitual sins, and ways of thinking/acting that hold me back from experiencing God's abundant life and the ability to walk in freedom? Which hand-me-downs are you wearing?

Just know that you are in good company. Read what the apostle Paul wrote in the Book of Romans about his own struggle:
I do not understand what I do. For what I want to do I do not do, but

what I hate I do. And if I do what I do not want to do, I agree that the law is good. As it is, it is no longer I myself who do it, but it is sin living in me. For I know that good itself does not dwell in me, that is, in my sinful nature. For I have the desire to do what is good, but I cannot carry it out. For I do not do the good I want to do, but the evil I do not want to do—this I keep on doing. Now if I do what I do not want to do, it is no longer I who do it, but it is sin living in me that does it.

So I find this law at work: Although I want to do good, evil is right there with me. For in my inner being, I delight in God's law; but I see another law at work in me, waging war against the law of my mind and making me a prisoner of the law of sin at work within me. What a wretched man I am! Who will rescue me from this body that is subject to death? Thanks be to God, who delivers me through Jesus Christ our Lord! **Romans 7:15-25**

Paul, as well as Jesus' disciples, struggled with sin. They fought against the world, the flesh, and the devil regularly. While we are not sure which struggles may have been visited upon them from their ancestors, the fact remains, that they had to rely on the Lord to give them to grace and power to overcome them.

Much of our struggle with sinful tendencies and patterns comes from wearing the hand-me-downs given by our parents. They most likely gave us similar ones to the ones they were given, and sometimes worse. That is why it is crucial that we take the time to ask our living relatives for their help in our discovery.

A good question to ask when they disclose some trait in themselves or another relative is, "Why do you think you/they acted that way or chose to behave like that?" This, or something similar, will help you not only discover an issue/trait (good or bad) but also uncover "where" it may have come from. When you go to a doctor because you are suffering from regular migraine headaches, it is not enough for the doctor to agree that you have headaches. You want him/her to tell you where the headaches are coming from and how to get them to stop.

Don't settle for discovering that your parent and/or grandparent suffered from insecurity, depression, or addiction. See if you can also uncover "why" they did. This will provide important clues as to how to best approach finding freedom yourself.

Remember, this process is not about assigning blame to anyone but simply to help identify the likely origins of both the positive and negative influences and iniquities in your life.

Afterward, if you will take the time to get alone with God and humbly ask Him to reveal any patterns/influences that may be hiding in the closet, or you are unsure about, He will eagerly speak to you and bring His light and wisdom into those shadows.

Just because your great-grandfather was an alcoholic, doesn't necessarily mean you are under a generational curse of alcoholism..... but, God may lead you to deal with that anyway. If both your grandfather and your father were alcoholics, abusive, or depressed - the evidence is more convincing that they have handed that iniquity/bent down to you. But remember, just because they left you a comfortable, warm flannel "shirt" in the closet, doesn't mean you have to wear it.....or that you must pass it on to your children.

If you are truly honest with yourself and reluctantly admit you "kinda" have a leaning toward a particular iniquity, (attitude, emotion, action) - ie. "anger" and the first thought that pops into your mind is -"but it's not THAT bad" or "THAT often", so "surely that isn't something I need to write down" - chances are the Lord is trying to bring it to your attention and the enemy is trying to minimize it and excuse/justify it away. I recommend writing it down. It is much better to deal with a molehill instead of waiting for it to become a mountain.

Leaving family for a moment, I also need to bring up other sources of significant influence (good and bad), and even curses, that may have shaped our lives to this point. These also need to be identified and dealt with. <u>We will unpack them in greater detail later</u>....

Word curses - These are words that have great power to influence our lives for good or for evil. Negative, hurtful, demeaning, and crushing words can stunt us and cause great damage to our souls. Positive words can motivate and energize us and our future mental well-being. These words typically come to us from people we care deeply about and respect, like parents, siblings, friends, coaches, teachers, and employers. Curses can also be spoken over us that we don't even know about and haven't even heard, such as from - evil strangers, practicing Satan worshippers, witches, and the like.
The tongue has the power of life and death - **Proverbs 18:21**

Agreements - may be considered as self-imposed curses. Agreements occur when we hear negative words spoken to us or entertain a lie from the enemy - and then agree with it - we accept it as truth.

Your coach yells at you, "You will never amount to anything" thinking he/she is going to motivate you to perform at a higher level, and in your heart/mind you say to yourself, "You're right, I probably won't". Or an angry parent says, "Why can't you be smart like your brother?", and you agree and tell yourself, "You're right, I am stupid". What about a parent who shouts, "You're just a selfish brat"..... even if there is some truth in their anger, your heart is deeply wounded by the harsh words from someone you are so close to, your mom or dad.

One true story that affected our lives deeply was that of a beautiful high school friend of one of our sons. She was naturally thin but seemed to be losing even more weight. When confronted in love about this, her response was as revealing as it was chilling. She said, "When I look in the mirror I hear a voice in my head telling me I am fat and ugly, and I need to lose weight". This type of lying, deceiving voice from the bowels of hell carries no weight, unless and until we agree with it. Once we agree, we begin to act upon our agreement. Always remember, what this young lady, fortunately, found out - *"the enemy comes to steal, kill and destroy"*. **John 10:10.**

Personal Abuse or Trauma - Horrible sins like neglect, and physical or emotional abuse at home or school can actually alter young brains and result in developmental and behavioral problems. Similar effects are seen in young people who have experienced trauma, like a serious accident or injury, the death of a parent, sibling, or friend, severe illness, and the like.

Lingering effects of these painful events include: increased anxiety, sadness, or even depression; increased anger or aggression; keeping distance between themselves and others; difficulty showing affection and an inordinate fear of death/dying.

Physical and Emotional Illness - A 2018 Swedish study found that individuals diagnosed with a stress-related disorder, such as depression, anxiety, paranoia, PTSD, addiction, obesity, etc. were much more likely to also be diagnosed with an autoimmune disease (rheumatoid arthritis, lupus, psoriasis, type 1 Diabetes, Crohn's, Celiac, multiple sclerosis, etc.) later in life.

• Younger people show even a higher correlation.

Stories abound of people who have found relief and healing from these disorders and diseases after finding freedom from their stress-related disorders in Christ.

Many (not all for sure) physical and mental illnesses can be caused by demonic activity handed down through our bloodline or made possible by giving the enemy a foothold in our own lives.

Luke 13:10-17 tells the story of Jesus healing a woman, crippled for 18 years, from a "spirit of infirmity". Other Bible translations use the phrases - "a disabling spirit" (ESV), "a sickness caused by a spirit" (NASB), or "crippled by a spirit" (NIV).

Mark 9:14-29 tells of Jesus healing a young boy who had suffered from a deaf and dumb spirit, as well as demonic-induced seizures, since childhood.

Matthew 9:32-33 Jesus heals a mute man who was demon-possessed.

Matthew 12:22 relates the story of Jesus again healing a man made blind and mute by a demon.

Matthew 4:24, John 5:1-8, Mark 5, and Matthew 8 remind us that not all sickness is caused by a demon.

Occult or Demonic Activity - Evil or Satanic activities, no matter how "innocent" you think they may be, can open the door for demonic activity in our lives, and give the enemy the permission to establish a stronghold in our lives. Examples include - horoscopes, ouija boards, seances, tarot cards, astrology, fortune tellers, and divination (**Exodus 20:3-5**). God declares He is a jealous God and will not tolerate His people having other, false gods. Any god or idol, or counterfeit source of "knowledge, wisdom or direction" is not of God and therefore, demonic.

The following passages will provide additional evidence that these practices are an abomination to God and severely punished:

Deuteronomy 18:9-14
Leviticus 19:31, 20:6 and 20:27
2 Kings 23:24a
1 Samuel 28:3
Revelation 21:8

Many have discovered that even watching horror movies, especially those with Satanic or demonic themes has unknowingly opened them up to nightmares, fears, and strongholds of the enemy.

Self-Inflicted Wounds - The Bible tells us of behaviors and choices that we make throughout our lives that will bring hardship, clarity, and even curses upon ourselves, Such as:

• Dishonoring parents - **Ephesians 6:1-3** specifically says that if as a child you decide not to obey your parents, a) "things will not go well with you", and b) "you will not enjoy long life on this earth" as consequences. The devil didn't bring this upon you - you did.

The Book of Proverbs is filled with practical wisdom regarding how we will reap what we sow as a result of our decisions and actions. Many are influenced by our ancestral "bents" no doubt, while others by the enemy of our souls - but we have a huge role to play in the quality of our lives depending on the personal choices we make along the way.

I will include a more expansive list of generational iniquities, sinful patterns of behavior, and curses in **Appendix B**. Highlight which ones obviously apply to you at first glance, and visit the list again after seeking God's insight and guidance.

Resist the enemy's lying voice suggesting one or more don't apply, are not that bad, or aren't a problem. He will also tell you this is a royal waste of time and it will do no good to go through this time-consuming exercise, so you may as well forget it. But, if you forget it, or go through it half-heartedly, or partially dishonestly (hedging) - you will not gain freedom in the area(s) you truly desire. Partial freedom is great, but you may leave the door cracked open for the enemy to continue to "devour" your life.

After you have made an honest go of the lists, it will then be time to move on to the next important step.

CHAPTER 7

CONFESS, REPENT, RENOUNCE

Unconfessed sin is one of the primary sources of generational iniquities. These may include actions, or patterns of behavior that have been normalized or hidden within the family but are contrary to God's Word.

Whoever conceals their sins does not prosper, but the one who confesses and renounces them finds mercy. **Proverbs 28:13**

As you walked through the lists you no doubt became more aware of habits, patterns, attitudes, and actions that are keeping you bound up and unable to enjoy the abundant life promised to God's children.

As the old saying goes, "How do you eat an elephant? One bite at a time". We need to be somewhat systematic and approach our issues one bite at a time. Let's start with your current hand-me-down wardrobe before moving on.

By following these next steps, in faith, you will begin to see chains fall away and freedom arrive. Be aware also that you may not always "feel" the heavy load fall away, but in most cases there is some immediate relief as the weight is being unloaded. More relief will come in the more entrenched areas as you continue to wrestle through them.

Your grandparents may have struggled with anger issues. Your parents may have inflicted great emotional damage on you with their words and actions when you were young. Now, you realize that you, too, have followed suit and hurt other people with your words as well.

We will deal with your ancestors later, but for now, you must confess your sin and renounce your participation in those iniquities, as well as the other iniquities you have participated in, or find present in your personality or lifestyle. Things like:

- addictive habits - alcohol, drugs, porn
- occult activities - horoscopes, tarot cards, ouija boards, etc.
- abusive language and word curses

You get the idea. God will be faithful to reveal those that need the most attention today, and others over time.

Whether the iniquity is from your ancestors or not, the first step in gaining freedom over it is to <u>confess</u> it as sin, <u>repent</u> of your involvement, and <u>renounce</u> your participation in it. You can't blame the devil or pass it off as "just a family trait". "It's just the way our family is", or "just the way I am" can't be used as a cop-out.

You are not personally responsible for the sins and iniquities of your ancestors. They may have provided a weakness or bent, but you made the choices to involve yourself in them and are totally responsible for the consequences of those choices.

If we claim to be without sin, we deceive ourselves and the truth is not in us. If we confess our sins, he is faithful and just and will forgive us our sins and purify us from all unrighteousness.

If we claim we have not sinned, we make him out to be a liar and his word is not in us. **1 John 1:8-9**

To "confess" basically means "to agree with God" that some words, actions, habits, inclinations, attitudes, etc. are sinful and grievous to God and to others.

To 'repent" means "to turn around and walk the other way", to "change your mind, heart and will by turning away from sin and returning to God".

To "renounce" means to "forsake" or "quit". Typically, by speaking aloud.

Part of our confessing and renouncing our sins and iniquities is taking the opportunity to bring those unsanctified and unholy thoughts/actions under the rule and Lordship of Jesus. If you are struggling with immorality, lust, etc. - first confess your involvement, repent of that involvement, and verbally renounce your participation in it. Next, you will want to bring those iniquities to Christ and place them under His Lordship. Do the same with each one on the list.

Here's a sample prayer to get you started....

Father, forgive me. I confess I have been offering myself over to the sin of _____, and now it has enslaved me. As hard as I try, I cannot rid myself of it. I repent and renounce my involvement in it Father, and by the cleansing power of your blood, I declare today that _____ no longer has power over me or my family after me.

> *More specifically, "I renounce my sexual sins. I present my sexuality to you, Lord Jesus, and present the members of my body to You as instruments of righteousness.*

I renounce every way I have given myself over to this sin. I consecrate my life [and this specific area] once more to the Lordship of Jesus Christ. Thank you that His atoning blood covers my sins and cleanses me. I am no longer a slave to _____, but a slave to righteousness.

Thank you for your forgiveness and mercy. Thank You that this sin is separated from me as far as the East is from the West and when you see me, you see the blood of Jesus.

Thank You for the freedom I have in you. Help me to walk in that freedom by the power of your Spirit living in me. I ask all of this in the matchless and powerful name of Jesus, my Lord.

Obviously, confessing, repenting, and renouncing your involvement in all the iniquities on your list will take time. Don't you think it will be worth it though - to be free from the bondage, the guilt and shame, and the constant accusation of the enemy?

Don't fall victim to the enemy's voice that will try to convince you that "you are just speaking words", "your heart isn't in this", "you don't really mean it", etc. He and his minions will stop at nothing to get you to stop this exercise and give up. They know, and hopefully, you do by now, that those words you are speaking carry the full weight, power, and authority of the Lord Jesus himself.

James 4:7 is just as true as **John 3:16**. You either believe it or not. You either act upon it or you don't.

*If you resist the devil, he **will** flee from you.* **James 4:7**

By renouncing and confessing (out loud) your involvement in these sins and iniquities, you are resisting the influence and power of Satan in your life, and he **WILL** flee. That doesn't mean he will leave you alone for the remainder of your life (**see Luke 4:13**), but you will experience great freedom as the strongholds of the enemy begin to crumble - see **2 Corinthians 10:4.**

Confessing, repenting, and renouncing don't have to be loud, dramatic exercises. There is no need for groveling or penance either - but simply speaking your heartfelt confession to God and also renouncing your being complicit with the world of darkness.

If we confess our sins, He is faithful and just to forgive us our sin and cleanse us from all unrighteousness- **1 John 1:9**

IF we confess, He WILL forgive and cleanse. It goes without saying, that if we DON'T confess, He WON'T forgive and cleanse. That's why this is so important.

So, what about our ancestors?

As God's beloved son/daughter, He sees, loves, and shepherds you as an individual child of His. He also sees your family bloodline. He created them and by His hand, your marriage and family were designed and brought together. He knew you "before you were even created" (**Jeremiah 1:5**) so He obviously knew your ancient ancestors, your recent ancestors, and He even knows the generations that will follow you - personally and intimately.

We must know then, that He knew your great-grandfather was an alcoholic, as was your grandfather. He knew your mom would struggle with addiction, anger, and depression.

Guess who else was watching all along and could see the family bent toward those particular sins? Do you think our arch-enemy wouldn't take any opportunity to "visit" those same iniquities on you and your family?

We must conclude therefore that God knew you would be "visited" by those ancestral iniquities. Thankfully, He has orchestrated this opportunity for you to not only learn about them but to do something that will not only provide you with much-needed freedom but set in motion that same freedom for the generations after you.

You, as a child of God, covered by the blood of Jesus, have the authority and opportunity to bring your entire family history/genealogy under the blood of Jesus as well. The curses and patterns of generational iniquities can stop with you - today.

See why this is so very important? See, also why the enemy doesn't want the church to walk in this truth

What can wash away my sin?
Nothing but the blood of Jesus.
What can make me whole again?
Nothing but the blood of Jesus.
Robert Lowry (1876)

CHAPTER 8

FORGIVENESS – FAMILY

Who is a God like you, who pardons sin and forgives the transgression of the remnant of his inheritance? You will not stay angry forever but delight to show mercy. You will again have compassion on us; you will tread our sins underfoot and hurl our iniquities into the depths of the sea. **Micah 7:18-19**

The Lord is compassionate and gracious, slow to anger, abounding in love. He will not always accuse, nor will he harbor his anger forever; he does not treat us as our sins deserve or repay us according to our iniquities. For as high as the heavens are above the earth, so great is his love for those who fear him; as far as the east is from the west, so far has he removed our transgressions from us. **Psalm 103: 8-12**

I, even I, am he who blots out your transgressions, for my own sake, and remembers your sins no more. **Isaiah 43:25**

Their sins and lawless acts I will remember no more. **Hebrews 10:17**

How would you feel if you fully knew that all of your past, present, and future sins were - hurled into the depths of the sea - separated from you as far as the East is from the West - and God would blot them out, and never remember them? Think about that for a minute.....

Well, if you truly believe God and that His Word is true - you have no other choice than to believe it. Once you confess your sin, bring it under the sacrificial blood of Jesus, He "is faithful and just to forgive it and cleanse you from it". From that point on, when God looks upon you, He sees Jesus and His shed blood.

With that in mind, we move on to three important elements involving forgiveness:

1. <u>Forgiving your ancestors</u> - every one of our ancestors was born a sinner and separated from God. They may have repented and given their lives to Jesus somewhere along their journey and brought their sins and iniquities under His blood. But, it is also true that many of them never did. They may continue to live in bondage to sin and its consequences today.

Whether saved or not, they were most likely unaware of the painful consequences their iniquities would have on their children and their children.

If you discover that one or more of the iniquities and sins you struggle with was/is also a struggle for a parent, grandparent, or even great-grandparent - you need to take the opportunity to forgive them.

Forgiving them is not an opportunity to assign blame, but to show mercy and obey Christ's words when he told his disciples:

Forgive us our trespasses as we forgive those who trespass against us.
Matthew 6:12 (Lord's Prayer)

For if you forgive other people when they sin against you, your heavenly Father will also forgive you. But if you do not forgive others their sins, your Father will not forgive your sins. **Matthew 6:14-15**

Father, forgive them; for they know not what they do. Luke 23:34 (see also Stephen's prayer in **Acts 7:59-60**)

Jesus really drove home the point by telling them (and us) this parable in Matthew **18:21-35:**

Then Peter came to Jesus and asked, "Lord, how many times shall I forgive my brother or sister who sins against me? Up to seven times?"

Jesus answered, "I tell you, not seven times, but seventy times seven.

"Therefore, the kingdom of heaven is like a king who wanted to settle accounts with his servants. As he began the settlement, a man who owed him ten thousand bags of gold was brought to him. Since he was not able to pay, the master ordered that he and his wife and his children and all that he had to be sold to repay the debt.

"At this, the servant fell on his knees before him. 'Be patient with me,' he begged, 'and I will pay back everything.' The servant's master took pity on him, canceled the debt, and let him go.

"But when that servant went out, he found one of his fellow servants who owed him a hundred silver coins. He grabbed him and began to choke him. 'Pay back what you owe me!' he demanded.

"His fellow servant fell to his knees and begged him, 'Be patient with me, and I will pay it back.'

"But he refused. Instead, he went off and had the man thrown into prison until he could pay the debt. When the other servants saw what had happened, they were outraged and went and told their master everything that had happened.

"Then the master called the servant in. 'You wicked servant,' he said, 'I canceled all that debt of yours because you begged me to. Shouldn't you

have had mercy on your fellow servant just as I had on you?' In anger, his master handed him over to the jailers to be tortured, until he should pay back all he owed.

"This is how my heavenly Father will treat each of you unless you forgive your brother or sister from your heart."

Pretty obvious, right? If we want to be forgiven, we better forgive.

Your relatives "trespassed against you", but, as Jesus and Steven both knew, "they knew not what they were doing" - meaning they had no clue the generational damage those iniquities would cause or how God was going to use them in your life and witness.

You have to forgive them for handing down iniquities they were not capable or willing to overcome themselves.

By not overcoming their anger, adulterous ways, addictions, etc., they allowed those iniquities free reign to be visited upon you and your family after you. If they were not believers, they had no choice but to perpetuate the sin they were held captive by. Knowing these things should offer us some degree of compassion and mercy as we bring those issues to the throne of Jesus.

Some iniquities, however, were visited upon us more personally, more tangibly, and possibly more painfully, by those people we loved the most - our immediate family. One or more of our parents, grandparents, aunts, uncles, cousins, etc. may have said or done something to us when we were young that has impacted our physical, emotional, and spiritual life more than anything else.

Whatever the offense, we are still commanded by Jesus to forgive. A monumental task, if not impossible, without the power of the Spirit and the love and mercy of God.

First, a word about forgiveness.....

You must know that forgiving them for their sinful attitudes, words, and actions does **NOT** mean:

- <u>You will no longer feel the disappointment, hurt, or betrayal by what happened</u>. You will most likely be reminded of it in some way when you hear other people share similar stories. You won't be able to stop the feelings from rising when you watch a movie, hear a song, or even hear a sermon that touches that wounded place in your soul. But that doesn't mean you haven't forgiven.

- <u>You can ignore/forget what was said or what happened</u>. Unlike God, we are incapable of totally forgetting or ignoring the hurtful things that people have said to us or done to us. Over time, God heals and memories fade, but they do not disappear. We can choose to never bring the offense up again or use it against the offending party but don't put the unrealistic expectation on yourself that you must forget what happened - but, you must still forgive...because He said to.

- <u>You only need to forgive once</u>. Because you continue to feel, and can't truly forget, you have to know that you may be reminded of certain iniquities from now on, and so you will need to use these opportunities to thank God for the multiple times He continues to forgive you and ask for the grace to give your offenders the same forgiveness and mercy.

- <u>God will not deal with that person</u>. We must let go of the natural desire for "payback". It is not up to us to make sure our offender is called out or made to pay for their sin - except in the case of physical or sexual abuse. Any illegal offense should be made public immediately and you should distance yourself from that person. God is the judge and He knows what happened. We must choose to allow God to determine the most appropriate course of action and leave that up to Him.

- <u>We continue to make it easy for the offender to hurt us again</u>. Forgiveness doesn't mean you put your physical or emotional life in jeopardy. Regarding any type of physical harm or abuse - flee. Get away and go to a safe environment. Protect yourself from further emotional distress and harm by setting clear boundaries and rules for future interactions, ie: not "arguing/discussing via text", we need to meet face to face and have a respectful, adult conversation. Consider a mediator and/or meeting in a public place to help mitigate harmful emotions.

- <u>You cannot pray for them</u>. A true sign of forgiveness is being able to pray for whoever hurt you. It is only by His grace that you can get to the point that Jesus and Stephen did, and ask God to forgive them. By praying, you are humbling yourself before God and allowing God to do what He knows is best in everyone's lives.

"But, if I'm honest - I really don't want to pray for them, or bless them - I want payback - I want to get even".

That's the battle we really fight in our minds when it comes to forgiving, right? We have to remember that forgiveness isn't optional for the Christian. We are commanded to forgive in the same way we are commanded to love - like Jesus.

By forgiving, we are making a conscious decision to cancel the debt we feel we are owed because of their offense. And yes, it seems impossible, but He is more than able to help us through it - if we let Him. And the consequences of not forgiving are far more damaging.

◆ Remember, God said if we choose not to forgive, He will choose to not forgive us.
◆ If we choose not to forgive, we will put in motion a new iniquity (unforgiveness) in our family that will be passed down.
◆ The opposite of forgiveness is judgment. By not forgiving we take on the role of judging them, and according to Romans 2 - that is not a good decision.
◆ Unforgiveness (the willful refusal to forgive and the harboring of anger, bitterness, and resentment toward someone) allows the enemy to establish a stronghold (a high place or place of authority) in your life which becomes the breeding ground for all manner of sin, and bondage.

In your anger (over injustice) do not sin. Do not let the sun go down while you are still angry, and do not give the devil a foothold (by nurturing anger, holding a grudge, or cultivating bitterness).
Ephesians 4:26-27 AMP

So, what sin tendencies, attitudes, habits, and vices can you trace back to your parents or beyond? Go back through your list and highlight those.

For the sake of simplicity, let's call them: generational and present day. "Generational", meaning - issues like anxiety, depression, poverty, and adultery - that have crippled family members in the past but aren't currently a struggle for you or your immediate family. "Present day" would be those generational iniquities that you identified that are current struggles for you, your spouse, and/or children.

That is where you start to pray.

Here is a simple template to get you started. Listen to God and expand this as He leads...

Generational - *Father, more than anyone else, You know the generational iniquities of _____ that have plagued my family for decades, and maybe longer. I come to You now to bring all those iniquities, lifestyles, and sins under the cleansing blood of my Savior, Jesus. I forgive my parents and forefathers for allowing these iniquities to pass down to me. I renounce them as sin and today I severe any hold they have on me, my wife, and all future generations of ours. I further declare this day that none of these sins will hereafter affect my family bloodline as they are now under the redeeming blood of Jesus. All curses are broken, and all works of the enemy are destroyed. Thank You Jesus for becoming a curse for us and for making provision by Your blood, for my bloodline to walk in freedom. All praise and glory to You, Lord.*

Present Day - After praying the above prayer for past generational sins and iniquities, take the time to pray more specifically for those sins and iniquities from your parents or grandparents that are still negatively impacting you and your family.

• Take one at a time and bring it before the Lord. Rather than rushing through the list by combining them in a category, such as "I confess my sexual sins", it is vital to confess your involvement in each one on your list and repent from it. ie: immorality, adultery, pornography, same-sex attraction, etc.

Father, even though I am not responsible for the sins of my parents and grandparents, I do confess that I have willingly participated in many of the sins and iniquities they have struggled with. Specifically, Father, I confess and renounce my involvement in _____, and ask that You please forgive me and cleanse me from that unrighteousness. I further declare this day that _____ will not hereafter affect my family bloodline as it is now under the redeeming blood of Jesus. All curses are broken, and all works of the enemy are destroyed. Thank You Jesus for becoming a curse for me and for making provision by Your blood, for my bloodline to walk in freedom. All praise and glory to You, Lord.

• At the end of your list, or wherever you choose to pause because of time, add this part of your prayer....

I ask Father, that You help me to walk each day forward in the power of Your Spirit, and give me the awareness and conviction to "resist the devil" when tempted to pick back up the sin I leave at Your feet today.

Remind me to "be alert" to my prowling enemy and to "put on the whole armor" You have provided me. Keep me diligently in Your Word and allow me to walk as the royal child that I am in You.

Thank You that I have been given authority "over all the power of the evil one", and "mighty weapons" to defeat him with. By Your might, allow me to walk in victory as I use them in battle.

Thank You for Your forgiveness and mercy. I ask all of this in the powerful name of Jesus and for Your glory. Amen

CHAPTER 9

FORGIVENESS – OTHERS

Then Peter came to Jesus and asked, "Lord, how many times shall I forgive my brother or sister who sins against me? Up to seven times? Jesus answered, "I tell you, not seven times, but seventy times seven. **Matthew 18:21-22**

While we would agree that unforgiveness is - "the willful refusal to grant forgiveness and the harboring of anger, bitterness, and resentment toward an offender", it is also an invisible umbilical cord that keeps us connected to the people and the pain from our past.

Much of the ground Satan gains in a believer's life is the result of unforgiveness. This becomes the breeding ground for all manner of sin. Family or not, if we want to: a) walk in obedience to God's Word, b) experience emotional and even physical healing, and c) break free from Satan's bondage - we have to forgive.

"But I don't want to" - not an option.
"But he/she doesn't deserve it" - not an option
"But I just can't" - not an option
"But what about them?" - not an option

If we profess to be a Christian, a follower of Jesus, we must obey His command, and forgive - period. There are no good, acceptable, Biblical reasons to not forgive.

Forgiving others will most likely include: family, friends, acquaintances, work associates, bosses, teachers, coaches, instructors, counselors, social media followers or trolls, and more.

Throughout your life, people will say things to you, say things about you - or maybe not speak at all. They will do things that hurt your feelings, make you mad, damage your ego, crush your self-esteem, exasperate you, mistreat or reject you.

What do we do with all that?

Chances are, no matter your age, you can still vividly recall someone's words and/or actions that wounded you deeply. So much so, that psychological studies have shown the physical responses (increased blood pressure and heart rate, muscle tension, etc.) of patients made to recall hurtful scenes from their past. Over time, the harmful effects of those words and actions can even lead to physical and emotional problems.

The "invisible umbilical cord" mentioned earlier stays attached until it is broken through forgiveness.

All of the comments mentioned in Chapter 8 regarding the necessity of forgiving our parents and grandparents, hold true for this category as well. After dealing with family, it is time to widen the net and specifically identify others in your life that God is bringing to mind that need to be forgiven.

As you read the following list, pause, think, pray - and ask God if there is anyone that He is prompting you to deal with. Here we go.....

Stepfather/mother/family
Brother
Sister
Cousin
Uncle
Aunt
Family friend
Teacher/Principal/Counselor/Advisor
Student
Boyfriend/Girlfriend/Fiance'/Ex-spouse
Coach
Instructor
Therapist
Doctor
Boss
Colleague
Client
Pastor/Church Leader
Friend/Acquaintance
Social Media "friend" /follower
Stranger

_____

_____

You may think of more, but this will give you plenty to start. As you identify someone from the list (even if you think it isn't "that big of a deal"), stop and pray the following prayer over them. If someone comes to mind......... he/she isn't there by accident.

Father, I ask You to please forgive _____ for _____.
You know the hurt they caused me, and I am trusting You to help me to walk
in Your forgiveness towards them. I release _____ to you and bring
all their hurtful words and actions under the blood of Jesus, and severe any
power they have over me and my heritage. I release _____ from any
thoughts of justice, vengeance, or pay-back, and declare that justice is Yours
and You will deal with them as You see fit.

By the authority given to me as a child of the King, I demolish any
stronghold the enemy has built in my soul because of their words and
actions and cancel any influence the enemy has had over me. I am free today
because of the blood of Jesus and the conquering power of His resurrection.
Help me to walk in the Spirit and in the freedom Your forgiveness brings. In
the mighty name of Jesus. Amen.

Now, right when you thought you were through with this category of forgiveness - I will remind you that there is yet another area of "Others" we have failed to mention.

There are words, prayers, and curses that others may have spoken over you that you are completely unaware of. I became aware of these years ago when a young woman began frequenting our church. As the worship leader in that church, I was asked to join the pastor one afternoon to pray for this woman. Come to find out, she was a recently converted witch and was obviously dealing with strong resistance to that decision. Over multiple prayer sessions with her, she told many hair-raising stories and provided some information regarding the mindset and practices of her former demonic community.

One such insight was that their members regularly met to pray - but, to pray *against* the things our church was praying *for.* They would pray for the destruction of churches, church leaders, marriages, families, unity, love, and the list went on. I have to admit, I was shocked.

There were multiple groups of people in our own community gathering to pray against God's people and call down curses on us? Who knew? I had been very naive.

Knowing this, I think it is a good idea to also include a prayer to cover any and all word curses that may have been spoken over you and your family by anyone unknown to you. Sounds weird I know, but covering all the bases is crucial.

Father, if there have been curses pronounced over me and my family line, I take this opportunity to once and for all break them, in the name of Jesus Christ and by the power of His blood. Satan has been defeated and disarmed, and his curses have no authority or power over me and my bloodline. I declare that, as a child of Almighty God, I am free from any evil pronounced over me and I have been given authority over "all the power of the evil one" in Christ. All curses are now broken and I walk in complete freedom in Christ. In the powerful name of Jesus. Amen.

CHAPTER 10

FORGIVENESS – ME

Sometimes the hardest person to forgive is ourself. As you will see in a minute, Satan uses guilt and shame to plant the thought in us that we are not deserving of forgiveness, or that what we have done is too big for God to forgive. And, as usual, it is a big, fat lie from the pit of hell.

We all would do ourselves a huge favor by re-reading the stories of men and women in the Bible who messed up royally. These people are in God's Word to show us real-life examples of people who sinned and were not only forgiven but significant in God's kingdom. Be sure and spend some time reading about:

Moses
King David
Jonah
Rahab
Peter
Mary Magdalene
Paul

I'm pretty sure you will discover that your mistakes, your bad choices, and your outright sin pales in comparison to theirs. I hope you are deeply moved by God's forgiveness and restoration of these fellow followers.

The honest truth is this - we are ALL going to sin. We have been freed from the curse of sin and the power of sin, but we are frail creatures whose flesh is very weak. God, in His mercy and by the sacrificial blood of Jesus, has forgiven us and filled us with the power to resist temptation and sin every day through His indwelling Spirit. The problem is most of us don't avail ourselves of His power and fail to walk in the Spirit moment by moment each day.

So, we will stumble along our journey in this life. And when we do, you can bet your bottom dollar our enemy, the devil, will quickly pounce. He will immediately speak words of accusation and defeat to us, and try his best to get us to slide down the rabbit hole of defeat, failure, unworthiness, doubt, fear and above all, shame.

Two tactics we must get ready to wrestle with are -

ACCUSATION

Then I heard a loud voice in heaven say: "Now have come the salvation and the power and the kingdom of our God, and the authority of his Messiah. For the accuser of our brothers and sisters, who accuses them before our God day and night, has been hurled down. **Revelation 12:10**

One of the many descriptive titles given to our enemy is "accuser of the brethren". He accuses us of failure, wrongdoing, hypocrisy - you name it - not only before God but in our own minds. And, he does this relentlessly, "day and night", meaning 24/7/365.

We are all familiar with his accusing voice. He tempts us to sin - we sin - he immediately speaks to us that we are "failures", "hypocrites", "probably not even saved", and more. You've heard him, haven't you?

So why would our diabolical enemy take so much time and energy accusing God's people? I think his end game is to slowly wear us down, to the point where we just give up. If he can get us to stop trying to hear from God or obey Him, then he will have accomplished a great victory. He knows he can't "un-save" us, but he is very capable of making our lives miserable and fruitless in the meantime. If we are ineffective witnesses for our God, lifeless, hopeless, joyless, and bound up by our enemy - he has reduced us to the same level as unbelievers - not believing in the grace and mercy of our forgiving Father God.

Another significant scheme of the enemy is to use accusation to try and overwhelm us with guilt and shame. Because of sin, all of us enter this world guilty. The Holy Spirit convicts us for our sin and moves us toward God, while guilt and shame are powerful tools in our enemy's arsenal that keep us feeling disqualified, flawed, powerless, not good enough, worthless, and failures as Christians. He uses guilt to make us feel bad about <u>what we have done</u> - but he moves us toward shame to make us feel bad about <u>who we are</u>. That is where he really causes destruction.

Once again, if we don't know or believe God's Word, we open the door for the enemy to torment us. We insult the work of Jesus on the cross by continuing to live in guilt and shame for our sins. Jesus suffered the curse for us; our sins are forever covered by his redeeming blood; he bore our guilt and shame (**Galatians 3:13-14 and Titus 2:14**) so stop condemning yourself. Those sins are gone, under the blood - the punishment for them has been paid, and they are not held to our account ever again.

The remedy for winning this battle in our mind is once again, imitating what Jesus did when He was accused by Satan himself. Immediately call a lie a lie, and counter it with the truth of God's Word. Chapter 3 provides you with much of the Scriptural ammunition you need to combat Satan's lies with the truth.

As believers and children of the King of Kings, we are no longer "sinners, saved by grace", but "saints, forgiven by God and covered by the redeeming blood of Jesus". We have to remind our tempter that God has freed us from all guilt and shame from our sins, and no longer sees or remembers them.

For though we live in the world, we do not wage war as the world does. The weapons we fight with are not the weapons of the world. On the contrary, they have divine power to demolish strongholds. We demolish arguments and every pretension that sets itself up against the knowledge of God, and we take captive every thought to make it obedient to Christ. **2 Corinthians 10:3-5**

God has given every one of His children weapons with "divine" power with which to "demolish" (utterly tear down, destroy) every "argument" and "pretension" the enemy proposes against the truth of God. These are the lies and accusations put forward by the enemy (the father of lies) to keep us under the paralyzing burden of guilt and shame because of sin. He will work overtime to convince us that we are not totally forgiven and that there is more for us to do than accept and appropriate the cleansing blood of our Savior.

It is up to us to "take those thoughts captive" and counter them with the truth of God's Word. Only then will we be able to walk in victory and freedom from these powerful schemes of the enemy.

AGREEMENTS and VOWS

Above all else, guard your heart, for everything you do flows from it.
Proverbs 4:23

For as a man thinks in his heart, so is he. **Proverbs 23:7**

Our mind ("heart") is the primary theater of battle in spiritual warfare. God knows it and repeatedly exhorts us to fill it with His truth and guard it above all else. Satan knows it also, and that is why he tries to control it through distraction, busyness, lies, accusations, and the incessant noise from our culture.

The other pathway Satan uses is frequently a byproduct of the first. When someone accuses you over and over of doing something or being something (ie: a loser, a failure, ugly, clumsy, stupid, etc.) there comes a point where you are going to be tempted to agree with them and accept their words as truth.

Sadly, I have personal experience with the devastation that Satan causes when we make agreements with his lies and accusations.

As a young teen, growing up without my father around, I clung to every word from those in authority over me, particularly my teachers and coaches. For the most part, my friends were always supportive but other peers were typically cruel and demeaning. My teachers were very supportive and encouraging, but my coaches were another story altogether.

Back in the 70s, coaches were at liberty to use more physical and verbal "motivation" as a means of achieving the behaviors and performance they demanded. I learned quickly that the coach's wooden paddle was very painful, so compliance with school rules was much easier to achieve. Athletics were different.....

Coaches were rough on us because their coaches were rough on them. They sincerely felt that physical and verbal "motivation" was going to produce superior effort by their players and result in more victories for them. With that mindset, they would regularly berate, demean, and expose us in front of our friends and teammates. Basically, they had the freedom to make our lives a living hell.

If that wasn't enough, they were also free to physically shove us, or grab our facemask and shake the stuffing out of us to make sure we heard their castigation - all the while cussing us up and down.

Sounds fun, huh? If you are an old coot like me, you probably are familiar with what I'm saying and may have some similar wounds. If you are a woman, you no doubt also have memories of your own from school, sports, etc. that still hurt.

The point is - I discovered later in life that I had made unconscious agreements with many of the abusive and demeaning things my coaches pronounced over me. Some that lingered were:

"You're a goat!" (*inferior performer*)
"You'll never amount to anything!"
"What a loser!"
"You're not good enough to be a starter!"

And that is a partial list. While their words and actions did actually serve to give me a kick in the pants and make me try harder, it seemed the harder I tried to please my coaches, the more difficult it was to achieve. Subconsciously, I found that I agreed with their assessment of me Thankfully, my senior year of high school we hired a new football coach whose style was the exact opposite of what I had been used to. He didn't cuss, he didn't shove and shake - he spoke encouragement and support, which served to motivate me like nothing had before. My senior year was awesome and my self-esteem got healed.

But, I had never broken the agreements I had made way back in high school. I found out after I got married, to my high school sweetheart, that I still had a sensitive wound. Whenever she said anything that I took as demeaning or non-supportive, I would lash back or withdraw. Even the tone of her voice would resurrect the inner thought - "you're a failure" (as a husband, father, or provider), "you will never be as successful as_____", or similar accusation.

As you can imagine, that served to put a strain on our relationship and a distance between us. Guess whose purposes that was serving? Not God's.

It wasn't until much later that God showed me that my self-worth had been damaged all the way back in middle school, and I had made agreements with Satan's accusations and lies. Until those were broken, and I truly understood who I really was in Christ, did my damaged soul receive healing. And you know what? About the time I felt that I had completely recovered from any feelings of inferiority or failure.... I lost my job in my 50s with kids in college and private school. My wife had to go back to work and I felt like a complete and utter loser...a goat...once again.

I vividly remember attending our small group meeting one night during that time. Our hosts lived in an extremely expensive part of town and had a wonderful home. As the men chatted in the kitchen before we got started, I became acutely aware of the conversation around me. Every man was talking about their latest success, their new vehicle, boat, vacation, etc., and there they were again.... Welling up from the recesses of my mind.... those old, familiar accusations - "you are such a loser", "your family will never have what theirs have", "you are a horrible provider", "your family could have done better with someone else". I got nauseous, and couldn't wait for it all to just be over.

Once again, Satan was circling back around and taking this "opportune moment" to press on my most painful bruise. He is relentless and will keep trying to find a way to immobilize you and put you on the Christian sidelines.

I bet you can remember something someone said to you that left a bruise on your soul. A parent, sibling, friend, colleague, etc., that deeply hurt you at the time, and it has honestly been hard to forget, much less forgive. Unless they are dealt with, even the most childish or seemingly insignificant comment or retort can leave lifelong damage.

We all try so very hard to fit in, to be accepted, popular, well thought of, respected, attractive, etc., etc. Do you remember the fear of possibly being picked last when you divided up into teams, or not at all? Growing up is hard to do.

Many times when we make agreements, we also make inner vows. Statements like, "I'll never let that happen again", or "No one will ever hurt me again", or "I will be the kind of father for my kids that I never had" are examples of vows we make with ourselves. The result of many of these vows is a natural consequence of the vow. Someone who vows never to be taken advantage of again, or hurt again will subconsciously erect emotional walls in relationships or become controlling in an attempt to have more control of the people and circumstances in their life. They become guarded, insensitive, and difficult relationally.

My vow to be the father for my boys that I never had, drove me to be "that dad" who coached every team, took off work early to spend time with the boys, and spent money I didn't have to try to keep up with the Joneses by given them vacations and gifts - all of which came at a high cost. The highest of which was the cost of not prioritizing the most important person in my life - my wife.

Thank the Lord for His mercy and protection, and for my patient, understanding, and long-suffering wife. Our relationship survived some bumpy roads, but God has more than restored what I damaged by following an inner vow.

We all have bruises, those tender places in our soul inflicted by family, friends, and others that, when pressed, trigger words and actions that aren't very Christlike. We have all most likely made some kind of inner vow along the way as well. That is why we need to take the time to search through the recesses of our minds and hearts and ask God to shine His light on any bruises that still exist, and any vows we may have made, however innocent. Then - we need to break those agreements. But how?

Similar to renouncing our involvement in generational hand-me-downs, we need to verbally renounce any agreements made with Satan's accusations. Secondly, we need to recognize whenever the enemy presents such thoughts (and he will), we need to resist it and counter it immediately with God's truth.

As the Spirit reveals past (and present) agreements to us, we start by breaking the enemy's grasp on us by means of those agreements. By agreeing with a word or a lying thought from the enemy, or strong negative feelings brought on by those words and thoughts, we inadvertently gave the enemy permission to torment us and keep us in bondage. Ask the Spirit to search you and reveal to you any times when you have said to yourself things along the lines of: "I am such a _____", "I'll never _____," "I'm so _____", "I always _____ or a host of others.

In addition to these, there are the agreements with sin itself: "I am just a worrier," "I am a drunk," "I am gay," or "I'm just a sinner". They can sometimes sound biblical but we don't want to be making agreements with our sin. The Word says we are dead to sin and alive to God. We are the dwelling place of the very Spirit of God. We are completely forgiven and dearly loved. As much as I understand the premise, I have to disagree with members of Alcoholics Anonymous continually declaring "I am an alcoholic" for the rest of their lives. Yes, they were alcoholics and addicted to alcohol, but if they are Christians, their identity is not "alcoholic" anymore.

Some agreements will be immediately obvious to you, while others will only surface with the help of the Spirit. Here is a sample, crafted prayer that you will want to modify to fit your unique situation.

[don't stop naming them until you can't remember any others]

Holy Spirit, search me, know me, reveal to me the agreements I have been making in my heart. I renounce the agreements that....
_____, _____,

_____, and _____.

Father, forgive me for giving place in my heart to these agreements. I confess them as sin and ask that you cleanse me now by the blood of Jesus, my Lord. I break these agreements in the name of Jesus Christ. I renounce every claim I have given the evil one in my life. I bring the blood of Jesus now against any spirits operating in me or any of the strongholds they have set up in me.

Specifically, Lord, I bring the blood of Jesus against all spirits of _____, of _____, of _____, [and so on]. I banish these enemies from every aspect of my life now. I resist the devil here and now and I command these spirits to flee in the name of Jesus Christ my Lord.

I am Your beloved child, Father, and a joint heir with Jesus himself. I am royalty, and will no longer agree with any words or accusations to the contrary. Thank You that in Christ I am forgiven and cleansed from all my unrighteousness. In the powerful and healing name of Jesus. Amen.

- -

The more times we have given our consent to the devil's accusations and lies, the more time it will take to untangle the web of deception in our hearts. Painful things have been said and done to us. Satan has used hurtful, wounding words, rejection, teasing, and outright lies of other people to "steal, kill, and destroy" our self-worth, and shape our personality. Ultimately, we feel alone and doubt God's love and plan for us.

By renouncing and severing our agreement with the enemy's accusations, we begin to recover precious areas of our hearts and experience the joy of walking in freedom.

We can't afford to "just bury it", because these evil lies will continue to resurface in our minds and assault us over and over again. We must take the time and effort to deal them a mortal blow. There is power...in the blood. Jesus' blood cleanses us from all sin and shame.

All of it.

CHAPTER 11

SUIT UP

If you have also renounced all the ancestral iniquities God revealed to you and forgiven your family, others, and even yourself - whew! - that is huge! You are already beginning to experience relief and freedom and are significantly down the road to throwing out the old hand-me-downs and experiencing complete freedom from the enemy's harassment.

As we have mentioned before, our enemy is conniving and relentless. Like he did with Jesus, he will flee when commanded to, but he will diligently be watching and waiting for another opportunity to trip you up. That is why God already made provision for us to win all of our future confrontations.

Those provisions include:

- Authority of all the power of the evil one - Luke 10:19
- Divinely powerful weapons to wield in battle - 2 Corinthians 10:4
- An army of fellow soldiers to fight with - Matthew 16:18
- Impenetrable armor to protect us - Ephesians 6:13-18

Each one of these is a book in itself, but I want to spend some time unpacking a very familiar passage. You could say this passage is TOO familiar. Most Christians know of it and can quote most or all of it. The trouble is - most of these same people don't actually DO what they are being exhorted and warned to do......put the armor on.

It is very clear in verse 11, that we should put on this armor *so that* "you may be able to stand against all the schemes of the devil". We can reasonably conclude by this statement that, if we choose **not** to put on the whole armor of God, we will **not** be able to stand against the schemes of the devil".

As Christians, we should assume that if we are exhorted to put on armor, we must need it. We must need it because we are being assaulted, and we are being assaulted because we are at war. Shouldn't we all know that? Shouldn't we be concerned about walking through our day on a battlefield in our street clothes? How utterly ineffective is a soldier who doesn't even realize a war is going on?

Our first defense in fighting this war has got to be - awareness. Far too many Christians are losing their battles and living defeated lives simply because they are not fully aware that the war declared upon us by Satan himself (**Revelation 12:17**) ions ago, is still raging all around us.

With that in mind, let's see why this armor is so very important. See **Ephesians 6:10-18**.

The Apostle Paul, the author of this powerful letter to the church in Ephesus, was very familiar with soldiers and their uniforms. In fact, he was imprisoned at the time of this writing. Most commentators believe he also spent 5-6 years of his life under arrest and about half of that time in an actual jail/prison.

Given the military connotations of this passage and the focus on armor, most believe Paul received his inspiration from closely observing the attire of his Roman guards. Paul's Ephesian audience was also intimately familiar with Roman soldiers - not to mention their familiarity with demonic ritual, paganism, and idolatry in their very pagan, Satanically-influenced city.

Finally, be strong in the Lord and in his mighty power.

• Our first admonition is to be strong in the strength and power of the Lord, not our own. We will fall every time we forget this and rely on our own abilities. We have no strength or power great enough to battle our ancient foe or any of his demonic hordes. *Great is our Lord, and mighty in power.* **Psalm 147:5. See also Jeremiah 32:17.**

Therefore, put on the full armor of God

• We are not told to put on whatever piece of armor we like best or is the most comfortable. God knows that we need the entire suit of armor to be successful in battle. Our enemy will exploit any exposed area of our life. Every piece serves a vital function and complements the others.

• Also, note that it is our responsibility to put the armor on. God doesn't do it for us. We are solely responsible for taking the time and making the conscious effort to put it all on. How often, you ask? How often do you put on your regular clothes? How often do you want to be able to <u>resist</u> the enemy and <u>stand firm</u> against his schemes?

Stand firm then, with the belt of truth buckled around your waist

• Soldiers of that day typically wore a long, loose-fitting, tunic as an outer garment which made running and close fighting/wrestling difficult. In preparing for battle, the soldier would first pull up his garment, tuck it back between his legs, and either tie the two ends together back around his waist in the front or tuck the material into his belt. His belt was a wide, sturdy piece of leather embellished with metal plaques that denoted status. A soldier's belt was both a symbol of his identity and a status symbol. Only a soldier could wear such a belt.

- The belt was a crucial piece of gear for the soldier. It served to support the soldier's back while also carrying his money purse, daily rations, dagger, and sword. Since most of their battles were fought in hand-to-hand combat, these smaller weapons were the ones primarily used.

- Some translations use the phrase "gird your loins" when referring to the act of "girdling" yourself for battle. According to the Collins Dictionary, to "gird your loins" means to prepare to do something difficult or dangerous.

With the breastplate of righteousness in place
- The breastplate (*lorica*) served as protection for the soldier's most vital organs, the heart, lungs, and other essential organs, both front and back. Therefore, if a soldier did not wear his breastplate, he was vulnerable to an attack that could result in instant death. The breastplate was typically made of bronze, metal mesh, and/or leather and weighed as much as 30 pounds.

With your feet fitted with the readiness that comes from the gospel of peace.
- Soldier's footwear (*caligae*) in Jesus' day was a leather, open sandal or boot designed for comfort and functionality. Their design allowed the soldier to work, march, and stand in them for long periods

without discomfort. The thick soles of the sandals were fitted with studs or hobnails designed to provide traction and protect his feet over rough ground.

Take up the shield of faith
* The shield (*scutum*) carried by the Roman soldier in battle was composed of multiple layers of wood glued together, often covered with additional layers of leather, all trimmed with a metal trim. The curved, rectangular shield measured some 4 feet long and 3 feet wide, in order to provide full-body coverage, and could weigh up to 20 pounds.

* The soldier's shield was not just defensive. Most also had a metal protrusion fastened to the middle of their shield that was used effectively to strike an opponent. The shield was also used to press forward into their opponents and push them back.

Take the helmet of salvation
* One of the most critical pieces of the soldier's uniform was his helmet. Each man's helmet was handcrafted from iron or brass and did a great job of protecting his skull, face, and neck. Each helmet was custom-made to fit the soldier's head and weighed some 10-15 pounds.

Additional padding was added to protect his brain from shock and for comfort.
* It goes without saying, that if a soldier didn't wear his helmet, he would not last long in battle.

The sword of the Spirit, which is the word of God
* The soldier's sword (*gladius*) was a stabbing sword for up close, hand–to–hand combat. The double-edged blade and sharp tapered

tip could also penetrate enemy armor making it a very deadly close-in weapon.

- This was a short, one-handed sword, 24 – 30 inches long and weighing about 3.5 pounds. This design was ideal for close combat and super effective in battle.

And pray in the Spirit
- Prayer isn't a physical piece of armor. It is, however, the most powerful of all weapons. Engaging the power of Almighty God allows the believer the opportunity to overcome all foes.

There are a multitude of scholarly interpretations regarding the spiritual significance of God's armor, but allow me to add a few of my own.....

Finally, be strong in the Lord and in his mighty power.
After instructing and admonishing his readers regarding their marriage, family, and work relationships, Paul concludes with "finally"..."let me tell you how to do these things" (my interpretation). Paul knows intimately that the only way a believer can follow the Lord's instructions for living is to rely on His strength and power. He follows immediately with a warning and another admonition because he also knows intimately that there is a diabolical enemy hell-bent on keeping all believers from living in the way he just outlined.

Therefore, put on the full armor of God.
You have probably heard that if you see the word "therefore" you need to ask, "what is this there for"? In Paul's case, he is drawing his audience's attention back to the two verses he just wrote - *Put on*

the whole armor of God, that you may be able to stand against the wiles of the devil. For we do not wrestle against flesh and blood, but against principalities, against powers, against the rulers of the darkness of this age, against spiritual hosts of wickedness in the heavenly places.

Therefore (because of what I just said), put on the whole armor of God. Part of the armor is not enough. We can put on the breastplate and not our helmet - and die. We can pick up a shield and a sword - and die. We need all of it - the whole armor of God in order to be victorious in battle. Also notice the armor is not our armor, but God's. He provides it and He empowers it. The army of enemies mentioned in verses 11 and 12 are far too many and too powerful for us to think we can defeat them in our own might.

The tone of Paul's words warns us that wearing the armor is not optional. The battle rages 24/7/365 and we are harmfully naive to think we can live victoriously and enjoy the abundant life without it.

Stand firm then, with the belt of truth buckled around your waist.

Paul's use of stand firm is Greek for "stand fast against an enemy, as opposed to running away". The Roman army soldier was forbidden to run away from a battle, and cowardice was a capital offense, punishable by death. It is interesting to me that the first thing we are told to do is hike up our comfortable tunic, tuck it in between our legs, and stow it in our belt. We need to get ready, suit up, and tighten our belts for battle.

That supportive and functional belt is referred to the "the belt of truth". In battle, truth holds us together and allows us the freedom to fight unencumbered. Believers must not only know the God of truth, but also the truth concerning who we are as His children, and the authority and weapons we have been given. Knowing this, we will not only be able to stand our ground in the midst of battle, but we can go on the offensive and overcome our enemies.

The belt that makes us battle-ready is the belt of truth. Not our truth, not the world's truth, but God's truth. His truth is what prepares us to fight and win our spiritual battles. Without it, we will become victims to the opposite of truth - Lies. Our enemy is well known as "the father of lies". (**John 8:44**) The ultimate defense against any attack of the enemy is our knowledge and understanding of God's Word. (see Chapter 3)

With the breastplate of righteousness in place.

Covering our most vital organs, and especially our heart, is the breastplate of righteousness. Since our own righteousness is considered "filthy rags" (**Isaiah 64:6**), Paul must be talking about Christ's righteousness. As we discussed earlier, the blood of Jesus cleanses us from all sin and we are considered righteous in Him. His righteousness protects our hearts from the onslaught of accusations and lies our enemy hurls at us daily. If we aren't sure of our righteous standing before God, we will be vulnerable to making agreements with them and acting accordingly. "We have been made the righteousness of God" in Christ and by His blood. **2 Corinthians 5:2**

All believers possess Christ's righteousness through our faith in Him but we are also called to display righteousness in our lives through our obedience to His Word. The enemy will exploit any weakness, personal sin, or unrighteousness for his advantage, and to our demise. Unconfessed sin leaves us vulnerable to spiritual attack. We must keep short accounts regarding the sin in our lives and quickly confess them and repent.

With your feet fitted with the readiness that comes from the gospel of peace.

Paul's mention of footwear was most likely a reference to the sandals worn by Roman soldiers. Much like athletic cleats today, Roman soldiers wore sandals studded with "hobnails" that provided sure footing and traction in battle. These "shoes" are a vital piece of armor needed to provide the believer with stability to stand in battle. The peace of Christ anchors us in times of trial and uncertainty. Our enemy knows that if he can steal our peace, he will be better able to knock us off our foundation. His goal is to affect our circumstances in ways that tempt us to be unstable, shaken, and defeated. If he can succeed in doing that, he will keep us on the defense, defeated, ineffective, and powerless as a Christian.

Our sandals of *peace* ("*shalom*"= wholeness, completeness, inner resting) ensure we are ready to deal with whatever Satan sends our way. The inner peace of Christ allows us to stay grounded, and sure-footed in the midst of fluctuating circumstances. The opposite of this peace would be "anxiety or worry", which the Bible plainly tells us are not from God.

We often cannot understand why we feel such peace in the midst of chaos. **Philippians 4:7** explains, *And the peace of God, which transcends all understanding, will guard your hearts and your minds in Christ Jesus.* This peace, God's peace, even though we may not be able to comprehend why we have it, still protects us and guards us (our heart/mind) from the enemy's relentless assaults, and grounds us in the battle.

His peace is so powerful, that we are even told to let God's peace "referee" in our decision-making as believers. In **Colossians 3:15**, we are told to, *"let the peace of Christ rule (umpire/referee) in your heart"*.

In sports, the referee/umpire makes the decision as to what "is" - whether a pitch is a ball or strike; whether a runner is safe or out; where the receiver caught the pass, etc. The peace of Christ is to "make the call" in our decision-making. We face dozens of decisions every single day, some small, some larger, and some potentially life-changing.

If we bring our thoughts and decisions under His rulership in our lives, He will calm our hearts/minds by giving us peace. When His peace is present, He is ruling and directing. When it is not, something, or someone, else is. When we are controlled by anxiety or worry, and a lack of peace, it is as if we have taken off our "peace sandals" and are unable to stand against the enemy's assault on our mind.

Satan's "peace", called the "world's peace" can offer you temporary distraction, deferral, or pleasure, but not lasting and meaningful inner peace. As attractive as pills, drinks, food, money, etc. may seem in the moment, they only serve to drag you deeper into the abyss the enemy has planned for your destruction. **John 14:27** reassures us - *Peace I leave you, My peace I give you; not as the world gives, do I give to you. Do not let your hearts be troubled, nor be afraid.*

The peace of Christ is our anchor. His peace gives us a solid footing in the battle against the forces of darkness. Without it, we stumble and fall. With it, we win.

Take up the shield of faith.
A soldier's shield provided significant protection from the weapons of his enemy. Whether blows from a sword in close contact warfare or the aerial assault of lethal arrows. As we have seen, the shield was his primary defensive weapon but could also be used offensively if needed. A shield kept the enemy's weapon from inflicting damage, but the force of the weapons could still be felt, and even leave a mark.

Our faith equips us with our largest and most formidable defensive weapon against the "fiery darts/arrows of our enemy". The enemy assails us up close and also out of the blue. Arrows are excellent weapons to launch from long distances so the target doesn't realize their imminent danger until it is too late.

Roman soldiers sometimes used flaming arrows against an enemy. These were typically longer, thicker, and heavier, so they had to be deployed from a closer distance. While the element of surprise was mostly lost, the impact of these weapons was significant.

The shield a believer must hoist in the presence of these powerful weapons is the shield of our faith. Our faith is not only in God but in the truth and power of His Word. His Spirit lives within us and with Him, we can do "all things". Because of our faith "no weapon formed against us will prosper" -that is, unless we drop our shield in battle.

I should add that even though the shied will protect our lives from flaming arrows, our shield will still feel their significant impact. We will most likely feel it as well, but we are not wounded because of our faith shield.

Take the helmet of salvation.

A soldier's head is his control center. If he cannot see or hear, he is at a significant disadvantage in combat of any kind. If he takes a blow to the brain, he is completely out of commission and possibly mortally wounded. The head must be protected at all cost. It is significant that Paul uses salvation to describe a warrior's helmet.

Our salvation is our most significant covering. No matter how difficult the battles, we are assured an eternity free from war, sickness, pain, hardship and death. We need not fear anything the enemy throws at us, because - we cannot lose. Without his helmet, a soldier faces certain death. Without salvation, the Bible says we are "dead in our trespasses and sins" (**Ephesians 2:1**). Our salvation, and all that has been given to us as a result, assures us of victory in any battle against our enemy. We are now adopted sons and daughters of the King of Kings, and joint heirs with Jesus. We have been given weapons, authority and a commission to use them in battle to push back the gates of hell.

But, if we have not experienced God's salvation, we are a soldier without a helmet or any of the other armor - and our outcomes are painful to consider.

And the sword of the Spirit, which is the word of God.

The soldier's sharp, double-edged sword was a most efficient and deadly weapon. It could easily penetrate the enemy's defenses and deal a mortal blow. Interestingly, Paul likens the Word of God to such a weapon. Paul also wrote in **Hebrews 4:12** that the Word of God is "quick and powerful, and sharper than any two-edged sword".

So, the conclusion we must draw is - the Spirit of God uses the Word of God to defeat the enemies of God and equip the children of God. If we are going to stand a chance of winning in spiritual warfare and experiencing the abundant life promised by God, we must know and wield the Word of God. Jesus showed us how to do just that in Matthew 4 when tempted by Satan himself.

If we don't know the Word, we can't use the Word. It is crucial to our victory and to advancing the gospel of Christ.
And pray in the Spirit.

In the heat of battle, prayer is our walkie-talkie to the General. Without it, we are clueless how to advance and best deploy our weapons and strategies to achieve victory. Prayer is also a dialogue, not a monologue. God desires to speak with us, to interact with us - if we will allow Him. We must learn how to pray, and move beyond the boring, powerless prayers we have grown up with. We must learn how to pray with power and authority and remove the mountains the enemy attempts to put in our path.

All that God is, and all that God has, is at the disposal of prayer. Prayer can do anything that God can do, and as God can do everything, prayer is omnipotent. R.A. Torrey

Until you know that life is war, you cannot know what prayer is for.
John Piper

CHAPTER 12

WARTIME MENTALITY

Dressing for battle is not an option for the Christian. It is essential, and we cannot expect to live an abundant life (John 10:10) or pass that legacy on to our children if we choose not to. The world is growing darker rapidly and the forces of darkness are gaining significant ground in our culture and even in the church. More than ever, believers need to step out from the lukewarm norm of "getting equipped" over and over again (with great information) - and get equipped and trained to fight a war. The equipment is great, but it doesn't do much good if you aren't in the game.

Let me ask -

Are you wrestling?
Are you winning?
Do you feel confident in your wrestling ability?
Are you proficient in using the "weapons of our warfare"?
Are you deploying them regularly?
Do you experience victory over sinful thoughts, emotions, and habits?
Do you wield your "sword" well in battle and in prayer?

Are you passionate about reading/knowing your Bible, or just try to have a brief "quiet time" whenever you can?

There are dozens of additional questions worth asking as well, but the truth is - most of us have to answer "no" to most of them. I was chief among us. For far too long, I knew a little about what the Bible said regarding spiritual warfare, but I was living in defeat regularly.

Like most church-going believers in the West, I knew a little warfare terminology ("Satan", "warfare", "enemy", "armor of God"), but had no clue how to use my God-given authority and weapons to fight and win this relentless war for my soul.

Whenever I have the privilege of teaching on spiritual warfare, the responses I most often receive are, "Where has this been?", "Why don't I know this?" and "I have been a Christian for years and have never heard this". That is what breaks my heart and fuels my desire to teach it.

We have lost the wartime mentality taught by Jesus and his disciples.

Do not think that I came to bring peace on earth. I did not come to bring peace but a sword. **Matthew 10:34**

For this purpose was the Son of God manifested, that he might destroy the works of the devil. **1 John 3:9**

The weapons we fight with are not the weapons of the world. **2 Corinthians 10:4**

In all these things we are more than conquerors through him who loved us. **Romans 8:37**

Put on the full armor of God, so that you will be able to stand against the devil's schemes. **Ephesians 6:11**

Submit yourselves therefore to God. Resist the devil and he will flee from you. **James 4:7**

And they conquered him by the blood of the Lamb and by the word of their testimony, and they loved not their lives even unto death. **Revelation 12:11**

The thief comes only to steal, kill, and destroy. I came that they may have life and have it abundantly. **John 10:10**

In addition to the hugely important process of Identifying, Renouncing, and Breaking all generational iniquities and sins, allow me to add a few thoughts concerning our need to maintain a wartime mentality.

1. **Stay Alert.** We are reminded to, *Stay alert and be of sober mind. Your enemy the devil prowls around like a roaring lion looking for someone to devour,* in **1 Peter 5:8**. Again in **1 Corinthians 16:13**, Paul warns us - *Be on your guard; stand firm in the faith; be courageous; be strong.* A wartime mentality is always watching, always battle-ready. This doesn't mean paranoid. There is not a demon under every bush or behind every negative thing that happens in your life - But, more often than not, we overlook the enemy's involvement in the people and circumstances he uses to anger, frustrate, and derail us. The Spirit inside us will give us discernment and alert us to the battle.... if we are listening.

Once we recognize we are in a battle, it is time to use the authority and weapons Jesus gave us to overcome the assault of the enemy and move on to #2.

We cannot afford to continue to enjoy the comfort of a Christian cruise ship when we have been called to kick down the gates of hell. We have been called to a battlefield, not a classroom. We have been entrusted with the very power of God's Spirit living inside us. We have been given (at great cost) divinely powerful weapons to fight with and Kingly authority to wield them. All come with a commission to go out and use them to defeat the enemy and walk in freedom for ourselves, our families, and others.

2. **Win your mind.** In all wars, there seems to be that one battle, the place where the tide of war seemed to turn and secure victory. Hastings, Yorktown, Waterloo, Gettysburg, Marne, Midway, and Normandy, were all battles that changed their respective wars. That battle in our lives is just as significant in winning the ongoing spiritual war. That is the battle for your mind.

While much more is covered in my book, <u>Victorious</u>, let me remind you what the Bible says about this all-important battlefield:

- *Therefore, preparing your mind for action and be sober-minded* **1 Peter 1:13**
- *Set your minds on things above, not on things that are on earth* **Colossians 3:2**
- *We demolish arguments and every pretension that sets itself up against the knowledge of God, and we take captive every thought to make it obedient to Christ.* **2 Corinthians 10:5**
- *Do not be conformed to this world, but be transformed by the renewing of your mind* - **Romans 12:2**
- *For the mind set on the flesh is death, but the mind set on the Spirit is life and peace* - **Romans 8:6**
- *But I see in my members another law waging war against the law of my mind* - **Romans 7:23**

· *For from within, out of the heart/mind of man, come evil thoughts, sexual immorality, theft, murder, adultery, coveting, wickedness, deceit, sensuality, envy, slander, pride, and foolishness.* **Mark 7:21-22**

Satan's attacks, temptations, accusations, and lies are mostly directed at our head - our mind. This battlefield must be secured. This battlefield must be won, or we have no chance of walking in freedom, health, and joy. Solomon, the wisest man who ever lived, said it best -

Above all else, guard your heart (mind). **Proverbs 4:23**. Above any and everything he could advise us to do - he told us to protect our mind, our thought life. Are we doing that? Do we have a strategy for doing that? If not - start today!

3. **Guard your mouth.** Another critical reason for guarding our mind/thoughts is - our words proceed out from there, and our words carry great power.

- *But the things that come out of a person's mouth come from the heart, and these defile them.* **Matthew 15:18**
- *Whoever would love life and see good days must keep their tongue from evil and their lips from deceitful speech.* **1 Peter 3:10**
- *The tongue has the power of life and death.* **Proverbs 18:21**
- *Gracious words are a honeycomb, sweet to the soul and healing to the bones.* **Proverbs 16:24**
- *The heart of the godly thinks carefully before speaking.* **Proverbs 15:28**
- *The words of the reckless pierce like swords, but the tongue of the wise brings healing,* **Proverbs 12:18**
- *In the same way, the tongue is a small part of the body, and yet it boasts*

of great things. Consider how great a forest is set ablaze by such a small fire. The tongue also is a fire, a world of evil among the parts of the body. It corrupts the whole body, sets the whole course of one's life on fire, and is itself set on fire by hell. Out of the same mouth come praise and cursing. My brothers and sisters, this should not be. **James 3:5-6 and 10**

There are just so many verses in God's Word about our tongue and the power of our words. As we have seen, our words have the power to inflict great harm on others as well as ourselves. Generations have been deeply affected for evil, and for good, by a fire set years ago by words spoken by grandparents and parents.

Another warfare mindset involving our words involves the words we proclaim in battle. With our words, we confess sin, we renounce involvement with generational sin, we forgive those who have sinned against us, and we exalt our gracious Father. We use other words containing the power and authority to rebuke and bind our enemy, resist temptation, and reject accusations and lies. Since Satan and his demonic words cannot hear our thoughts, we, like the disciples, must speak these words out loud in the authority of Jesus' name. **See Mark 16:14-18, Luke 10:17, Acts 3:1-6,16, Acts 4:8-10, Acts 4:29-31 and Acts 16:16-17.**

We should live each day with a heightened sensitivity to the power of the words we speak to others and over ourselves. We should also be quick to invoke the power and authority of Jesus by speaking His Words in battle. Nothing is more powerful in prayer than praying the Word of God (our sharp, two-edged sword). We need to be trained on how to pray from a foxhole, not a deck chair.

4. **Keep short accounts.** We can't fight well if we are weighed

down with the burdens of sin and unforgiveness. Jesus commands us to forgive "as He has forgiven us". How many times do you think He has forgiven us? Do you sin once a year? Once a month? I am pretty sure he is telling us to forgive frequently, to not harbor unforgiveness, or to put it off until we feel like it. Not letting "the sun go down" on our anger means - get over it before sundown...quickly.

We also need to keep short accounts when it comes to our own sin. Satan, our accuser, will be certain to bring our past sins up to us over and over and over again. He will try to ensnare us with the bondage of guilt and shame until we are bound, unable to fight him, and useless to the Kingdom. When we sin (and we will) quickly take time to confess it and repent, trusting God to be true to His Word - *If we confess our sin, He is faithful and just to forgive our sin and cleanse us from all unrighteousness* .**1 John 1:9**.

There is nothing else required of us. No penance, no performing acts of service, and no groveling. God is faithful and He will immediately forgive us - IF we confess. So be quick to ask for His mercy and forgiveness and move on, back into the battle, and walk in the Spirit. *Walk by the Spirit, and you will not gratify the desires of the flesh.* **Galatians 5:16**

5. **Pull Weeds** - As a hobby gardener, I learned quickly about weeds. Weeds blow in your garden from everywhere it seems. They are relentless. The only way to stay on top of them and not have them take over your garden is to pull them. Therein lies the technique. It is not enough to pull the tops off; mowing and weed eating disperses them and makes them worse; but leaving them alone is definitely not an option. They will grow and spread and choke out the plants you are trying to grow. Eventually, they will choke off the life-giving nutrients and starve the plant to death.

So, a gardener has a choice - take the time and effort (and it takes both) to bend down and pull them, or ignore them and hope they don't do much damage, and maybe they will just somehow go away. The only way to get rid of them for good is to grab them near the surface of the soil and slowly pull until they come out from the root. If you don't get the root, you will see them again soon and have to do it all over again.

See any similarity here with our subject matter?

Iniquities, curses, unforgiveness, guilt, shame, and all demonic influences are all types of spiritual weeds. They blow into our lives from "out of the blue" it seems, but they have actually been sent by a diabolical source. They take root in our mind (garden) and start to slowly grow. Over time they begin to impact the good spiritual growth we have begun to see in our lives. They take vital nutrients away from that growth and slowly start to choke off our spiritual health. If we leave them alone they will flourish and overwhelm us. Their main purpose is to "kill, steal, and destroy" our lives and our heritage.

6. **Call for backup**. Warriors have a much better chance of success if they fight together. A soldier alone on the battlefield is a sitting duck for a horde of enemies. Our first call on the walkie-talkie is to God. He is mighty in battle and more powerful than any enemy we face. He also said *"I will build my church and the gates of hell will not prevail against it"* (**Matthew 16:18**). He didn't say the gates of hell will not prevail against Rob (or John or Mary). The church body was created to be an elite, God-powered, army capable of prevailing against the enemies of God and mankind.

God urges us not only to pray and commit our burdens to Him, but to seek out others who will help us carry our burdens by their prayers. The Bible says, *"Carry each other's burdens, and in this way you will fulfill the law of Christ"* (**Galatians 6:2**).

There are times in battle when we need help. We may be wounded (spiritually, emotionally, even physically) and in dire need of fellow soldiers to have our back. We need others in our company to fight with us, and to fight for us. If you are not a member of a local, vibrant, Bible-believing church - join one. If you are not connected to other warriors who know how to pray powerfully and fight our enemy - join a small group or Bible study group.

Some battles are just too big to fight alone. Do NOT try to fight those battles by yourself. Call for backup. Do not be ashamed or embarrassed to ask for support. We all need it and there is much power in doing so.

If two of you on earth agree about any matter that you pray for, it will be done for you by my Father in heaven. **Matthew 18:19**

After they prayed, the place where they were meeting was shaken. And they were all filled with the Holy Spirit and spoke the word of God boldly. **Acts 4:31**

So Peter was kept in prison, but the church was earnestly praying to God for him. Suddenly an angel of the Lord appeared and a light shone in the cell. He struck Peter on the side and woke him up. "Quick, get up!" he said, and the chains fell off Peter's wrists. When this had dawned on him, he went to the house of Mary the mother of John, also called Mark, where many people had gathered and were praying. **Acts 12:5,7,12**

Find one or more prayer partners to walk through the battlefield with. We all need someone to have our back when we are under attack.

7. **Welcome True Friendship.** Peter had good intentions. He truly meant what he said when he told Jesus, *"Even if all fall away on account of you, I never will. "Truly I tell you," Jesus answered, "this very night, before the rooster crows, you will disown me three times." But Peter declared, "Even if I have to die with you, I will never disown you."* **Matthew 26:33-35**

We all have good intentions too, right? How many times have we sinned and promised the Lord, "I will never do that again"? Ever made a vow to start reading your Bible, have a regular daily quiet time, or read the Bible all the way through? I hope you have done better than me when it comes to following through with those promises.

Peter's "I've got this" mentality didn't work out too well for him either. Our passionate desire for independence, that "I can do it" mentality, comes automatically at birth, because of our sin nature. Toddlers have it, adults still have it.

Truth is - most of us fear becoming truly known by another person. It is a struggle (especially for men) to even let their walls down to be known by their wives. We often fear that "if he/she really knew us they wouldn't approve of us or love us, and we can't risk that". That would be evidence of another sinister sin we are all born with - pride - as a result, we hide. Much like Adam did after he sinned, we try to hide from God and from others, for fear of the consequences of being "found out". So we settle for surface-level relationships.

A true friend, on the other hand, is allowed to know us and then loves us anyway. Know why? Because he/she has issues and failures in their past also. None of us can point a finger.

One of the biggest problems with having "an accountability partner" is that the person holding you accountable needs accountability in areas of their life as well. Your "friendship" then is based on making much of your failures and the bad things you are doing, and nothing about your progress and growth. Accountability is good and should always be a part of a true friendship relationship - but not its entirety.

Authentic friendship has your back. Picking you up when you fall and fighting fiercely by your side in times of battle; kicking you in the pants when you need it and cheering for you when progress is made. What a gift from God.

But, as the saying goes - "to have a friend, you must be a friend". We have to be willing to accept someone's "warts and all" and not judge. We have to be the friend we are looking for in others.

When God links you with a true friend, you know it. In your spirit, you feel the love, acceptance, and freedom to finally be honest and open with someone who will keep your confidences, earnestly pray (fight) on your behalf, and never stop encouraging you. In the process, accountability becomes an unexpected byproduct.

Two are better than one because they have a good reward for their toil.
Ecclesiastes 4:9

"Iron sharpens iron, and one person sharpens another."
Proverbs 27:17

CHAPTER 13

WITH YOUR BOOTS ON

Hiroo Onoda was a Japanese intelligence officer who for **29 years** after the end of World War II continued to hide, fight, and kill in the jungles of the Philippines because he did not believe the war was over.

The vast army of "principalities, powers, and spiritual forces of darkness" (1/3 of the angels in heaven) are different soldiers. They all know the spiritual war is over, and they lost. The problem for us is - they get to stay on earth and wreak havoc until God says it's time for their final judgment.

In the meantime, they are mad as hornets. They know their time is short, and that Jesus has defeated them, so they are working 24/7/365 to try and take as many people into the pit of hell with them as they can. In addition, they work overtime to destroy the lives of all Christians, their marriages, children, finances, joy, peace, witness, and heritage.

Therefore rejoice, you heavens and you who dwell in them! But woe to the earth and the sea, because the devil has gone down to you! He is filled with fury because he knows that his time is short. **Revelation 12:12**

That is why Jesus said - *Do not suppose that I have come to bring peace to the earth. I did not come to bring peace, but a sword.* **Matthew 10:34.**

- Jesus was on a mission. -

The over-arching reason (mission) for Jesus leaving His throne in heaven, taking on the form of mortal man, and suffering a brutal death on the cross was this -

The reason the Son of God appeared was to destroy the works of the devil. **1 John 3:8**

We should obviously then take a look, and discover what Satan's "works" are. While this is not an exhaustive list I'm sure, it should help to give some understanding.

His "works" include:
- attempting a coup to overthrow God Himself, which got him kicked out of heaven
- successfully tempting Adam and Eve to abdicate their God-given authority to rule earth
- causing Adam and Eve to sin and ushering in the curse of sin on all humanity to follow
- trying to eradicate God's people through hardship, captivity, and war
- a failed attempt to kill Jesus shortly after His birth
- causing pain, heartache, disease, sickness, accidents, injury and death
- blinding the minds of unbelievers and stealing God's Word from their hearts
- crippling people with mental illness, demonic possession and torment

- inflicting mankind with mental illness, depression, anxiety, suicide, and the like
- fueling hatred, crime, war, and calamities of all kinds
- attempting to kill Jesus once and for all on the cross
- persecuting God's church and its leadership from the beginning till now
- destroying Christian marriages by multiple means
- mounting an ongoing campaign of lies, deception, and accusations against believers
- deceiving believers and the church into not fighting against him

I hope you get the point. His works are evil and they are many. But, Jesus destroyed them ALL on the cross - by His blood being shed and His triumphal resurrection from the dead! Someone should say, *Amen* here......

With His dying breath on the cross, Jesus said - "It Is Finished" - to announce to humanity and Satan and all of his minions.... "I won, you are all defeated and doomed to the fiery pit of hell for all eternity - and my followers will walk in freedom from all of your works". He not only saved us from the curse and penalty of sin - He saved us from being slaves to the kingdom of darkness for our lifetime.

The <u>future</u> for Satan and his armies is certain and secure. They will pay dearly and eternally for their evil. One day, you and I will never be bothered by them again, for all eternity!

Then I saw an angel descending from heaven, holding in his hand the key to the abyss and a huge chain. He seized the dragon—the ancient serpent, who is the devil and Satan—and tied him up for a thousand years. The angel then threw him into the abyss and locked and sealed it so that he could not deceive the nations until the one thousand years were finished. (After these things he must be released for a brief period of time.) NET **Revelation 20:1-3**

When the thousand years are over, Satan will be released from his prison and will go out to deceive the nations in the four corners of the earth—Gog and Magog—and to gather them for battle. In number, they are like the sand on the seashore. They marched across the breadth of the earth and surrounded the camp of God's people, the city he loves. But fire came down from heaven and devoured them. And the devil, who deceived them, was thrown into the lake of burning sulfur, where the beast and the false prophet had been thrown. They will be tormented day and night forever and ever. **Revelation 20:7-10**

The <u>present</u> for Satan and his armies is also certain and secure.

❖ **<u>They have been disarmed of their weapons and defeated</u>**

• *And having disarmed the powers and authorities, he made a public spectacle of them, triumphing over them by the cross.* **Colossians 2:15**
• Don't EVER forget - the only power Satan has over us is the power we give him!

❖ **<u>Jesus took back the authority that was given to Satan by Adam and Eve in the Garden</u>**

I pray that the eyes of your heart may be enlightened in order that you may know the hope to which he has called you, the riches of his glorious inheritance in his holy people, and his incomparably great power for us who believe. That power is the same as the mighty strength he exerted when he raised Christ from the dead and seated him at his right hand in the heavenly realms, far above all rule and authority, power and dominion, and every name that is invoked, not only in the present age but also in the one to come.

And God placed all things under his feet and appointed him to be head over everything for the church, which is his body, the fullness of him who fills everything in every way. **Ephesians 1:18-23**

❖ **Jesus paid the price for our redemption by His blood, canceling the curse and penalty for sin**

- For he has rescued us from the dominion of darkness and brought us into the kingdom of the Son he loves, in whom we have redemption, the forgiveness of sins. **Colossians 1:13-14**

In him we have redemption through his blood, the forgiveness of our sins. **Ephesians 1:7**

But now, in Christ Jesus, you who were once far off have been brought near by the blood of Christ. **Ephesians 2:13**

For He made Him who knew no sin to be sin for us, that we might become the righteousness of God in Him. **2 Corinthians 5:21**

We were therefore buried with him through baptism into death in order that, just as Christ was raised from the dead through the glory of the Father, we too may live a new life. **Romans 6:4**

❖ **Jesus gave His followers His authority to rule once again over the kingdom of darkness, as well as the weapons with which to rule**

The seventy-two returned with joy and said, "Lord, even the demons submit to us in your name". He replied, "I saw Satan fall like lightning from heaven. I have given you authority to trample on snakes and scorpions and to overcome all the power of the enemy; nothing will harm you. However, do not rejoice that the spirits submit to you, but rejoice that your names are written in heaven." **Luke 10:17-20**

For though we live in the world, we do not wage war as the world does. The weapons we fight with are not the weapons of the world. On the contrary, they have divine power to demolish strongholds. We demolish arguments and every pretension that sets itself up against the knowledge of God, and we take captive every thought to make it obedient to Christ. **2 Corinthians 10:3-5**

❖ **Jesus gave His followers marching orders (a commission) to move out into the world battlefield and use the authority and weapons He provided to set others free**

Heal the sick, raise the dead, cleanse those who have leprosy, and drive out demons. Freely you have received; freely give. **Matthew 10:8**

So, what is the bottom line to all this?

If we profess to be Christians, Christ followers, we have not been called to attend church once a week, give a little money when we can afford it, read our Bibles when we find the time, and try to be nice, moral boys and girls. Jesus came bearing a sword. He came to destroy an enemy's evil works. He came to fight, and He commissioned His people to do the same.

The problem is, that His people have been deceived, accused, lied to, and ensnared by the clever voice of our arch-enemy. We realize much too late that we are predisposed to the iniquities and sins of our ancestors. We have been crippled by listening to and agreeing with the relentless accusations and lies of the enemy. We are bruised and battered by an enemy who has stripped us of our armor, weapons, and authority - by simply hiding the truth in plain sight.

So brothers and sisters, it is time to suit up, grab your sword, and get in the battle. I can tell you, that it is a bit intimidating at first and a tad scary. We haven't had much practice in wrestling and warfare. Sadly, we have had few leaders brave enough to teach us and lead the charge. We also are in desperate need to learn to pray differently. Wartime prayer requires more than "now I lay me down to sleep", and "Lord, be with John today and help him have a good day" type prayers. We need to learn a new language of prayer, a wartime language filled with God's Word (truth, and sword), and invoking the most powerful name ever spoken - **_Jesus_**.

The church would do well to heed the words of the apostle Paul. "Look carefully then how you walk, not as unwise but as wise, making the best use of the time, because the days are evil" (**Ephesians 5:15-16**). If the days are evil, what are we doing about it? You know what I was doing? I was hiding out in my church, getting equipped, and learning new things. I am embarrassed to think how naive and cowardly I was for far too long.

The war is raging all around us. Believers are being wounded and taken to the sidelines every day for "lack of knowledge" and lack of fighting. Unincumbered by our generational hand-me-downs and the accusing voice of our enemy - armed with God's authority and mighty weapons - it is time we stand against the enemy's schemes and advance the cause of Christ.

We need to live with a wartime mentality - but not as frightened, reluctant soldiers but as confident, victorious liberators.

It's time we decide to go down swinging; to die with our boots on.... for His glory!

CONCLUSION

The bottom line is this - we are ALL affected, positively and negatively, by our upbringing and the people who were most involved in it. We have all been given hand-me-downs from our past, but we have also been allowed to decide which to try on and wear - and which to throw out.

We don't get to choose our genetic makeup. We don't have a vote in who our parents will be or what kind of job they will do raising us. We can't change the positive or negative decisions they made along the way or the emotional struggles they endured. Likewise, we cannot go back and "undo" what was said or done to us along the way, or the circumstances under which we were brought up - and the associated scars that may have resulted.

But, God can. He designed our genetic makeup. He chose our parents and family for us. He knew the teachers, coaches, and friends that would shape our lives and lead us to where we are today.

Whenever I find myself feeling like a victim or comparing my past to other people's - I have to stop and remember that God sovereignly orchestrated all of it. The good and the bad, and that He has promised to "work all of it together for my good" (**Romans 8:28**) if I will trust Him and walk with Him. I am not a victim, I am a victor.... in Him.

As a child of the King of Kings, forgiven and covered by the blood of Jesus, we have the authority and opportunity to throw the unwanted hand-me-downs away for good. Satan will ensure they are visited upon us, but, we can renounce, resist, and repel them by the authority we have been given in Jesus, and by His matchless name.

The sinful inclinations and actions, the emotional dysfunction, and the ongoing visitation of generational iniquities can stop with you - today.

APPENDIX A

Based on decades of competent research, there is a 100% chance everyone reading this book will die. What happens after that has been the subject of much debate since the beginning of human history. Some believe there is nothing after they die, they simply are buried and that is the end. Christians believe that God provides a way for people to live and thrive for eternity after their death here on earth.

The most significant question any human being can answer is just that - what do you believe about life after you die?

When I was a teenager, I heard a speaker make the following statement - "If Christians are wrong about eternity, and all life ends at death, then you haven't lost anything by believing in Jesus. But, if Christians are correct, and there is an actual heaven and hell and an eternity spent in one place or the other, then you have lost everything if you reject Him".

My conclusion, even as a teen was, "Am I willing to risk my eternity if I'm wrong? Shortly afterward, my mother came into my bedroom as I was going to bed one night and asked, "Honey, if you were to die tonight, do you know for certain that you would go to heaven or hell?"

Of course, I reassured her that heaven was the place for me, even though I had no clue if that was true. As God would have it, that same night I had one of the most vivid and frightening dreams of my young life. I dreamt of dying and being laid in a coffin (that seemed like a box). The box was then covered with dirt, and I laid there and laid there, and laid there. For an eternity, I just lay there, in the dark.

I woke up in an all-out panic. Heart racing, sweating - truly frightened. Well, that did it. I could take a hint. God was doing a wonderful job of getting my full attention. I crawled out of bed and knelt there. I said, "God if you are really real, and all of this is true - please forgive me and grant me eternal life. I believe Jesus died for my sins, and I give my life to You".

God doesn't always use dreams to gain our attention - but He does love us enough to gain it. We may experience the death of a friend, family member, or loved one; we may contract a serious illness, we may simply hear a convicting sermon or the testimony of someone we respect - but He always works to get our attention.

Instead, he is patient with you, not wanting anyone to perish, but everyone to come to repentance. **2 Peter 3:9**

If you have never made this most life-altering decision, maybe God is trying to get your attention here in Appendix A. Here is the truth according to God -

• You were born into sin

Behold, I was brought forth in iniquity, and in sin did my mother conceive me. **Psalm 51:5**

Therefore, just as sin came into the world through one man and death through sin, and so death spread to all men because all sinned. **Romans 5:12**

For all have sinned and fall short of the glory of God. **Romans 3:23**

- **You can't avoid it, change it, or work your way out of it**

No amount of good deeds, good intentions, church attendance, or prayers prayed can undo what was done in the Garden of Eden. Our sinful condition is not a result of what we have done - but who we are.

As for you, you were dead in your transgressions and sins, in which you used to live when you followed the ways of this world and of the ruler of the kingdom of the air, the spirit who is now at work in those who are disobedient. All of us also lived among them at one time, gratifying the cravings of our flesh and following its desires and thoughts. Like the rest, we were by nature deserving of wrath. **Ephesians 2:1-3**

- **Even though you are considered dead in your sin (separated from the life and blessings of God), Christ died on your behalf and paid the price for your sin - the shedding of blood.**

In him we have redemption through his blood, the forgiveness of our sins. **Ephesians 1:7**

But now, in Christ Jesus, you who were once far off have been brought near by the blood of Christ. **Ephesians 2:13**

For He made Him who knew no sin to be sin for us, that we might become the righteousness of God in Him. **2 Corinthians 5:21**

- **Your decision is whether or not you will accept His gift of salvation (saving you from eternal judgment/hell)**

For God so loved the world (YOU), that he gave his only begotten Son, that whosoever believes in him should not perish, but have everlasting life. **John 3:16**

Salvation is found in no one else, for there is no other name under heaven given to mankind by which we must be saved. **Acts 4:12**

For it is by grace you have been saved, through faith and this is not from yourselves, it is the gift of God not by works, so that no one can boast. **Ephesians 2:8-9**

It is God's grace that is awaking faith in you right now. That faith will allow you the grace to make the conscious decision to simply accept what Jesus has done for you and place your trust and your life in His hands.

· **Salvation is simply the act of declaring that faith and yielding your life to His leadership (Lordship) in your life.**

If you declare with your mouth, "Jesus is Lord," and believe in your heart that God raised him from the dead, you will be saved. For it is with your heart that you believe and are justified, and it is with your mouth that you profess your faith and are saved. **Romans 10:9-10**

Take a minute and pray this prayer, as an act of that faith:

"God, I confess that I am a sinner and in need of You. I ask that You forgive my sin and cleanse me from all unrighteousness in my life. Thank You Jesus for sacrificing Yourself on my behalf and releasing me from the curse of sin and death I was born into. I accept Your gift of salvation and ask You to be the Lord of my life from this point forward, to lead me, teach me, and protect me as I seek to follow You and bring You glory. Thank You for saving me today. In Jesus' name. Amen."

I am so very thankful for the Lord leading you to this book and to this Appendix. I pray the God of our salvation will make Himself real to you in the days ahead, and give you the desire to walk with Him, read and study His Word, and witness of His changing faith in your life.

Now - go tell someone about your decision and your new life in Christ.

APPENDIX B

WITCHCRAFT & SATANISM:

Spells - Rituals - Sacrifices - Incantations - Dedications - Voodoo - Horror

OCCULT:

Ouija Boards - Seances - Sorcery - Fortune Telling - Astrology - ESP - Hypnosis - Crystals - Charms - Computer or Board Games - Occult literature - Channeling - Spiritism - Psychic healing - Curses/Spells - Death wishes

MUSIC:

Occult or Satanic/Demonic themes or words - Rebellion - Drug-oriented - Overtly Sexual/Sensual - Rebellion - anti-God - Death themes/words

IDOLATRY:

Cults - Meditation - Yoga involving mantras/chants - Eastern religions - Secret societies/Orders - False Christian sects

DRUGS/ADDICTIONS:

Use of illegal substances - Alcohol abuse - Chemical dependency of drugs, prescriptions, smoking - Addiction to Food, Sex, Exercise, Work, Pleasure

SEXUAL SINS:

Pornography - Fornication - Adultery - Rape - Incest - Masturbation - Fantasy - Homosexuality - Beastiality - Pedophilia - Abortion - Abuse

REBELLION:

Disrespect - Disobedience - Controlling - Rebellion - Defiance - Profane - Sacreligious Blasphemous

VULGAR or ABUSIVE LANGUAGE:

Cursing - Off-color jesting or language - Cynicism - Hurtful - Sarcasm

ANGER:

Hatred - Rage - Malice - Bitterness - Resentment - Unforgiveness - Revenge - Judgmental - Blaming - Critical - Prejudice - Bigotry/Racism - Defiance

FEAR:

Fear of: Rejection - Failure - Exposure - Harm - Death

ANXIETY:

Worry - Lack of Trust - Despair - Hopeless - Lack of Control - Restless - Suicide

PRIDE:

Self-focus - Self-pleasure - Self-righteous - Showing out - Controlling